LANGUAGE, 'E
AND THE CURRICULUM

Peter Doughty

Schools Council Programme in
Linguistics and English Teaching

EDWARD ARNOLD

Other publications in the Programme

Language in Use
Language in Use Tape
Exploring Language

Printed in Great Britain by
Western Printing Services Ltd, Bristol

Contents

PAGE

Preface   5

PART I

Language in 'English': the development of a linguistic perspective on language work with the mother tongue

One The present condition of 'English'   7
    1. Introduction   7
    2. The 'progressive consensus'   12
    3. Problems in the practice of the 'progressive consensus' approach   16

Two Language as a focus for work in 'English'   24
    1. Current attitudes to language in the profession 24
    2. 'English', language and linguistics   29
    3. Linguistics, language study and *Language in Use* 31

Three The design of *Language in Use*   36
    1. An outline of the design   36
    2. Educational objectives   41
    3. Awareness, competence and the English class 48

References   50

PART II

'English' in the curriculum: an examination of the objectives, aims and approaches currently revealed by the work of the English class

One Public and professional attitudes to 'English' and their origins 53

Two The problem of describing the variousness of English practice 62

Three The English teacher's view of his task   69
    1. Basic categories   69
    2. Current views of aims and objectives 72
    3. Learning processes used by the teacher of English 78
    4. Approaches to 'English'   79

References   88

Bibliography   90

Appendix: Two units from *Language in Use*   93

THE SCHOOLS COUNCIL PROGRAMME IN LINGUISTICS AND ENGLISH TEACHING consisted of a team of twelve teachers and linguists working together at University College, London, between 1967 and 1971 under the direction of Professor M. A. K. Halliday, Professor of Linguistics at the college.

In 1970 Longman published *Breakthrough to Literacy*, which resulted from the work of the primary school section of the team.

Language in Use, written by the secondary team was published by Edward Arnold in 1971. This was more than just a book: it consisted of a loose-leaf volume presenting to teachers about 120 lesson units designed to help with language teaching over the whole range of secondary school age, and was accompanied by a tape for use with certain units. This was followed in 1972 by a collection of papers, also published by Arnold, entitled *Exploring Language*, which set out and discussed the theoretical background to *Language in Use*.

A series of papers in linguistics was commissioned from members of the team after the Programme had finished, and four volumes have been published by Longman. *Language, 'English' and the Curriculum* by Peter Doughty is closely linked with *Language in Use* and it was decided that Edward Arnold should publish the book as the final part of their series.

Preface

The two parts of this volume represent two of the three faces of curriculum research and development. The first is turned towards the teacher and his day-to-day problems in the class-room and is represented here by an account of the way in which one piece of development in the field of 'English' came to have a particular shape and focus. In the process, I have to say a great deal about current attitudes and approaches in English teaching. While this focus gives to Part I a general relevance to all those who are interested in the problems and practice of 'English', it also points towards the second face of research and development work, the question of the aims, objectives and approaches which teachers hold and make use of in a particular area of the curriculum. In Part II, therefore, I go on to explore what teachers of English accept as the purpose and direction of their work at the present time.

In one sense, it could be argued that this was a 'theoretical' rather than a 'practical' question and therefore less relevant to ordinary teachers in the class-room. I would suggest, however, that this is an unreal distinction. Knowing what you are doing and why you are doing it seems to me to be a very practical matter and this is what Part II is really about. It presents a view of aims, objectives and approaches which sees them as the features that really determine what a teacher does from moment to moment in the act of teaching. From this point of view, the choice is not a choice between a focus on the practicalities of the task and an exploration of theoretical questions, the implication always being that the teacher can safely leave questions of theory to those who do not have to grapple with the realities of the class-room: it is a choice between an explicit recognition of those things which actually shape decisions in learning situations and an implicit belief that we do know what we are doing and why we are doing it, so we have no need to talk about it.

The third face of research and development is turned towards the relationship between a design for some area of the curriculum, in this case the design of *Language in Use* for work in 'English'; and the intellectual foundations upon which it rests, in the case of *Language in Use*, the linguistic perspective on language which informs it. While much is said in Part I concerning this relationship, this volume is not the place for a detailed account of those foundations themselves, so the reader must be ready to look elsewhere, if he wishes to find out more about the particular linguistic perspective in question and the theory of language from which it derives.

Ideas grow out of many things, but most of all out of that free exchange of thought which only comes when a group of like-minded people trust each other enough to speak what is shaping in their minds. I owe a great deal to the occasions when I was privileged to be involved in such a group at University College London, a group which included at different times Professor M. A. K. Halliday, Professor Basil Bernstein, and Professor Mary Douglas. During that period I joined the team of the Schools Council Programme in Linguistics and English Teaching to help develop *Language in Use*, and from which I was commissioned to write this book. I owe much to the encouragement and sharp wit of my colleague, Geoffrey Thornton, and over the years to Professor James Britton and Nancy Martin of the London Institute, and to Douglas Barnes of the Leeds University Department of Education. I owe most, however, to my wife Ann, for her constant encouragement and acute criticism.

Manchester, 1973   Peter Doughty

PART I

Language in 'English': the development of a linguistic perspective on language work with the mother tongue

One   The present condition of 'English'

1   Introduction

The main focus of this part is upon the way in which a particular piece of research and development in the curriculum area of 'English' grew out of a particular situation in the teaching of 'English' and a particular perspective on language and its use. In order to show how the design of *Language in Use* was developed, it is necessary to look at attitudes to language work amongst teachers of English, as well as at the theoretical foundations of the design in a linguistic perspective on language. For this reason, it has something to say to all those involved, directly or indirectly, with the practice of English teaching, as well as those whose immediate interest is in the area of curriculum development.

It seems to me that, in the field of curriculum research and development at the present time, there are two main schools of thought, the 'grand design' school and the 'grass roots' school. The 'grand design' school believe that there is one true way of tackling a particular problem in the curriculum and that their task, as curriculum developers, is to discover it. Once discovered, they must then reveal it to the world and insist that teachers entirely remodel their existing practice so as to accord with its prescripts.[1] The 'grass roots' school, on the other hand, believe that there are as many true ways of solving a problem as there are experienced teachers meeting it in their day-to-day work. In this case, the task of the curriculum developer is to discover how these experienced teachers are tackling the problem and turn their answers into a form that can be given to other teachers.[2]

The 'grand design' school runs into difficulties, because practising teachers are seldom convinced that there is only one solution to a key area with which they are concerned. The diversity of the educational system in this country, and the very great differences in the attitudes and assumptions and capabilities of teachers and pupils throughout the country, would tend to reinforce the truth of this conviction. On the other hand, the 'grass roots' school run into parallel difficulties, because the answers they derive from teachers working in one situation do not necessarily recommend themselves to teachers who see themselves as working in a situation radically different.

In the process of developing the design for *Language in Use*, I came to see that neither school would meet the needs of this particular piece of research and development. In the event, both schools contribute to the design, but in such a way that the limitations of one are modified by the perspective the other provides. I want to begin, therefore, not with a 'grand design', nor with an account of 'grass roots' practice, but with the 'operational' objectives that were devised for *Language in Use*. Operational objectives are those goals that a research and development team devise, or rather, ought to devise, to guide the development of their design. They are to be contrasted with the 'educational' objectives which are relevant to the particular area of the curriculum that is under review. The educational objectives accepted for *Language in Use* are discussed in detail in Section Three.

Operational objectives are properly contingent, shaped by the immediate circumstances of the educational and curriculum context as the developer finds it. They are, therefore, 'constructs',[3] that is, they are formulated by the developer according to his reading of that educational and curriculum context and his assessment of his needs according to the work he has set out to do. In Professor Medawar's phrase, these operational objectives are an expression of a '. . . possible World'.[4] What he means by a '. . . possible World' is a hypothesis about some particular state of affairs. As far as this book is concerned, the particular state of affairs in question is the practice of English teaching in the late 1960s, its problems and needs. What these operational objectives assert, therefore, is one version of those problems and needs formulated from a linguistic point of view.

The general situation pertaining in a subject like 'English' at any one time, we can call 'the state of the art'. It may seem an obvious thing to say that this state of the art enters into the basic thinking of a team when they are working out their operational objectives. My reference to the 'grand design' school, however, is a reminder that this is not always accepted as necessary or desirable. There have always been those, from Plato onward, who have thought that educational practice and the curriculum ought to be shaped by anything rather than the state of the art at the time at which they were speaking.[5] My own view is that avoiding any consideration of the state of the art leads almost certainly to the production of materials which, however intrinsically valuable in themselves, have no power to influence, or to alter, the attitudes or practice of individual teachers, because the credibility gap between their practice as they understand it, and what is offered as the new way, is too wide for them to bridge.

It is for these reasons, therefore, that I begin by setting out the operational objectives for *Language in Use* and then go on and describe the climate of opinion amongst teachers of English at the present time. I am then in a position to outline the design of *Language in Use*, because that design must be seen against the background of a particular view of English, the view that I am going to call the 'progressive consensus'.

Underlying all four objectives is the idea that what an operational objective does for the curriculum developer is keep his eyes very firmly on the particular needs of teachers in the real situation of the class-room. I say this, because the objectives are here formulated in terms of what can be done to make life easier for teachers, and not in terms of the formal categories of a model. The value of such models, and what they can help us to achieve in rethinking our practice as teachers, I take up in the second part of this volume.

The first of our objectives was the provision of a guide to 'good practice'. The words available for talking about what teachers actually do are not very satisfactory. I do not myself like referring to a teacher's 'pedagogic', or his 'professional equipment', or his 'skills'. Of all the words available, 'practice' seems the least objectionable. It manages to convey the sense that the activity of teaching is a combination of experience, flair, know-how, and something which we might call at this stage of the discussion 'a teacher's view of his role'. Good practice, in English, then, refers to the activities and procedures which are accepted at present as those most likely to realise in the class-room the aims and objectives for English, as those aims and objectives are understood by the teachers most actively engaged in the field. Good practice, as an operational objective for *Language in Use*, therefore, is the requirement that it provide a practical class-room approach to the ways of teaching which are at present most often advocated as necessary and desirable for work in English. Moreover, it is a requirement that this guidance towards good practice be provided in such a way that it is accessible to anyone interested in using it. By accessible, I mean that whatever is offered ought to be set down in a public language. A public language is a language the full meaning of which is recoverable from the text alone. It does not depend upon the reader's having shared a common experience with the writer, nor does it expect him to empathise with the views, insights or projective personality of the talented individual, or group of individuals, who furnish the substance of the text.[6]

The second of our objectives was the attempt to offer an approach to one key area in the curriculum that would show how patterns of work could be *ordered* without being *structured*. This distinction seems to me a vital one for an area of the curriculum like English. Many of those who have been most active in recent discussions of English teaching have argued that English is essentially one area in the curriculum to which the notion of structure is entirely inapplicable. The root of their argument is that any kind of structured programme would so constrain the English teacher in his choice of what to do, and when to do it, that it would inhibit the proper development of the imaginative and creative side of his work.[7] It is this side of the work, moreover, which is to be regarded as the defining characteristic of English within the contemporary curriculum. The dilemma was that, in terms of day-to-day practice, 'unstructured' could so easily become 'totally directionless'. The distinction between an *ordered* and a *structured* approach offers one way out of this dilemma. The structured approach is the predetermined programme, designed and put together by someone who is not himself the teacher, and operated by the teacher without the latitude to modify elements in the course of his teaching it. On the other hand, the ordered approach is one in which the design or framework may well be worked out by someone who is not the

10

teacher, but the model used for the design is of such a kind that the teacher retains his essential autonomy when face to face with his pupils in the learning situation. Essentially, an ordered approach to English is one that sets out the options and then leaves the teacher in a position to make a clear and considered choice from what is available, according to the needs of the learning situation as he reads them.

The third objective came directly from the brief of the Programme in Linguistics and English Teaching. I have already said that our work was focused upon one key area of the curriculum. This key area was not the whole field covered by the teacher of English, but that part of the English teacher's work concerned with developing the pupil's understanding and use of his own language, his mother tongue. What we wanted to do was find a way of relating the insights into language offered by Linguistics to the practical problems of teaching and learning in the English class.[8] The most important consideration that this raised was the fact that the majority who might choose to use what we produced would not themselves have any familiarity with the field of Linguistics. It seemed to us that there was no sense in which we could consider preparing materials which required for their successful use a long period of training prior to their being taken into the class-room. The teacher had to feel able to pick up what we offered and start using it right away in the context of his ordinary day-to-day practice. As far as the pupil was concerned, we did not want to demand a particular analytical technique for the discussion of language. It did not seem consonant with current educational thinking for us to expect pupils to acquire an explicit technique of linguistic analysis before they could begin to explore their own language. Moreover, the acquisition of the kind of meta-language such a technique would make necessary was irrelevant to the needs of the majority of pupils, given our educational objectives.

The fourth and final objective relates to the difficult question of 'competence'. It seemed to us, given our third objective, that one thing we had to do was to provide teachers with a coherent approach to the whole question of pupils' growth in command of their language, both spoken and written. As I have written on this subject elsewhere,[9] I do not intend to enlarge upon what I mean by 'command of a language' in this context. The idea of competence, however, is discussed in Section Three, pp. 45 to 47. In accepting growth of competence as an objective, we were thinking in terms of pupils' ability to use language to live as much as their ability to use language for learning, that is, their effective operational competence in using written and spoken English within the context of the curriculum.[10] These two ways of using language come together, however, within this one operational objective, because there is an intimate relationship between the two. The growth of what most people understand by 'command of a language' for learning, the ability to write and speak English in ways that are publicly approved of within the existing school system, seems to us unattainable, unless there is an equal emphasis upon the growth of the pupils' 'command of a language' for living.

These four operational objectives were formulated through reference to the particular context of the state of the art in English. In particular, the selection of these objectives rather than any others was largely determined by the climate of opinion amongst teachers of English created by the advocates of the 'progressive consensus' approach. The next step in the argument, therefore, is an account of the attitudes and assumptions about English which inform the progressive consensus. Like all generalised pictures of a particular set of attitudes and assumptions, it is open to local and particular objection. Nevertheless, I do think it represents what at the present time leading opinion in this country, in the United States, and in Canada, accepts as good practice as far as the teaching of English is concerned.

2   The 'progressive consensus'

The progressive consensus is an approach to the teaching of English which has developed over the last decade and embraces a loose association of ideas, attitudes and assumptions about the work of the English teacher which have together radically changed its orientation. Elsewhere,[11] I have already discussed some of the ideological aspects of this consensus. What I want to focus on at this point is the way in which the consensus affects the English teacher's practice.

There are four features which currently differentiate the progressive consensus from the way in which we customarily think of most other subjects in the curriculum. Firstly, there is the question of *flexibility*. Teachers of English now have a very strong sense that whatever they

12

do in the class-room, whatever they choose to offer their pupils, must be very closely related, some would say related minute by minute, to the changing needs and interests and responses of the particular pupils with whom they are working.

Secondly, and following logically from this notion of flexibility, there is a very broad view of *the range of concerns* which it is possible for the teacher of English to focus upon. Formally, English is seen as having no 'subject matter', no body of data to impart.[12] It is as though English is seen as quite distinct from those subjects in the curriculum which have a 'content', and therefore require instructional or expositional methods of teaching. At its broadest, this view sees the work of the English teacher as encompassing anything which an individual teacher judges to be relevant to the needs of his pupils.[13]

The third of these four features really arises out of a combination of the first two, *flexibility* and *range of concerns*. This is the idea of the teacher's capacity for *continuous creativity* in the learning situation.

The individual teacher's desire for a continuous flexibility towards the learning situation in the actual moment of teaching, and his wish to bring within the compass of his professional review a very wide range of concerns, has led to an overwhelming emphasis upon his ability to 'write his own programme as he goes'. Much discussion within the general orbit of progressive consensus ideology suggests that a teacher needs to be able to plan his work from moment to moment, from day to day, according to the way the work goes. It is as though his whole teaching programme were one continuous heuristic. Strong advocates of the consensus approach go so far as to suggest that English, at the present time, is 'progressive' in so far as it alone amongst the subjects within the curriculum can create the conditions for a kind of 'serendipity', an element of happy chance that is essential to that freshness, that liveliness, and above all, that imaginative insight, without which activity in the class-room cannot properly be called learning. In terms of content, and of what pupils are asked to do with it, therefore, the ideal for the teacher of English, as it is presented by the progressive consensus, is a practice that is *continuously creative* in terms of the teacher's ability to invent and exploit for the benefit of his pupils an indefinite succession of unique learning situations.

Taken together, these first three features of the consensus necessarily lead to a fourth. In order to create the conditions for flexibility, range of concerns, and continuous creativity in the learning situation, the roles of teacher and pupil have to change radically from what they can be assumed to be in a situation in which it is axiomatic that the teacher is knowledgeable and the pupil ignorant; that there is an agreed content, an agreed progression through that content, and an agreed educational objective for the whole process, the transfer from the teacher to the pupil of a body of knowledge. This change of role requires the teacher to move from being an *instructor* to being an *entrepreneur* and a *consultant*: the pupil to move from being a passive *recipient* of information to being a *participant* and a *researcher*. While much has been said about the changes required of the teacher, those demanded of the pupil are equally important. Pupils can be as conservative in their attitude to the participation required of them in a learning situation as teachers are commonly accused of being. There is much evidence from the comments of individual teachers which suggests that pupils do find the role of recipient much easier to take up and perform than the alternative role of participant and researcher that is being offered to them in exchange.

It is these four factors, interacting upon each other, that have created the climate of opinion in English which I am calling the progressive consensus. From this perspective, the teacher will no longer spend most of his time expounding a body of information which he has himself acquired and carefully articulated in terms consonant with those acceptable to the discipline from which he acquired it. Instead, his energy will be directed towards the organisation of an indefinitely extendable variety of situations in which his pupils explore their own experience of the world. Hence we hear of 'working in groups', the 'English workshop', the 'thematic approach', 'getting outside the class-room', and so on. The teacher of English is required to construct the learning situation around the on-going activities and interests of his pupils. This is his entrepreneurial role. In order to do this effectively, however, he himself has also to become a consultant. He may initiate a particular sequence of work but, once initiated, he is there to suggest, hint and guide his pupils as they pursue it in their own terms. It must be said emphatically, however, that this does not mean he is passive towards the learning situation. Comment on the progressive consensus, basically hostile
14

to its whole ideology, has frequently implied that all the teacher does is stand around and let his pupils get on with it.[14] In fact, what the teacher has to do is relate to each of his pupils, or groups of pupils, individually, because they each present different needs in relation to the on-going pattern of work in the learning situation at different moments in its course. Taken seriously, this is a far more exacting role for the teacher than the one traditionally assigned to him. If there is a criticism to make, it is that some versions of the progressive consensus make so great a demand upon the teacher that only the most gifted can hope to meet them.

From a linguistic point of view, one of the most important aspects of the change of role required of the teacher is that he has to listen seriously to what his pupils have to say. In his traditional role as expounder and instructor he believed himself to be in possession of the facts and his pupils ignorant; consequently, 'listening to what his pupils had to say' was more a question of matching their 'answers' to his preconceived notions of what 'a right answer' would be like. In the new situation, what he has to focus upon is his pupils' particular needs at a particular point in the course of work which they themselves have planned. They will ask questions of him, questions to which there will be no one 'right' answer that he can give in reply, because the questions will be shaped by the immediate context of their asking. Correspondingly, he must listen in order to find out where the work is going, for he cannot operate with a preconceived notion of what the next stage of the work will look like. Taken as a whole, what this means is that the teacher is infinitely more vulnerable, infinitely more exposed to the pressures and changes of the learning situation, because the relationships which it now requires are necessarily personal rather than formal.

From the same linguistic point of view, the most important fact about the pupil is that he ceases to be a passive recipient of what is expounded and has to participate actively in the learning process. This means he is no longer free merely to sit at his desk, listening and recording, and returning at regular or rare intervals a predictable form of answer to a predictable form of question. He has to act, plan, discuss, organise and consult. Moreover, he has to do this, not as an isolated individual, but usually as a member of a group. The group may be as small as two members of a class or may include as many as a dozen or fifteen. Whatever is the case, however, he has

15

to operate in the learning situation as someone who relates continuously to a number of his peers. This means that he has to develop a whole range of social strategies for coping with the interaction involved. In effect, he has to be able to articulate the forms of social behaviour which Ervine Goffman calls 'performance'.[15] In particular, interaction of this kind means that he has to learn how to exercise control over others, through linguistic means alone; and he has to learn how to tolerate delay in expressing his own point of view while others express theirs. Both of these aspects of verbal interaction in a small group are likely to put a very real strain upon pupils.

The progressive consensus in English teaching requires, therefore, the establishment of a new set of social relationships for the classroom, between teacher and pupil and between pupil and pupil. A new set of social relationships necessitates the learning of new ways of speaking, the means by which those relationships can be realised through language.[16] Without the means to language them, the relationships cannot become '. . . concerted human activity'. This leads me to suggest that one of the major stresses which the use of the consensus approach may give rise to is primarily linguistic in origin. Learning how to language a new relationship is a *product* of that relationship. In other words, the learner must bear with the uncertainties of rehearsing a new way of speaking in order to learn how to use it.[17] Tolerance for such uncertainties is so unusual an occurrence in our educational system as it is at present organised that this need in itself would be enough to put many attempts at the consensus approach seriously at risk.

3 Problems in the practice of the 'progressive consensus' approach

The adoption of the progressive consensus as a basis for practice has led to much exciting work in many places, but it has also given rise to a number of difficulties. These difficulties, or limitations, in the approach as it stands at the present time for the most part arise out of the emphasis the consensus places upon flexibility, range of concerns, continuous creativity, and a changed pattern of relationships between teacher and pupil. The freedom of action for the teacher which this emphasis has created makes it necessary for him to work in a situation which makes enormous demands upon his professional expertise and his personality.

Five particular limitations influenced the design of *Language in Use*. The first of these concerns the teacher himself. At the very centre of the consensus approach is the notion of the teacher as someone who is capable of projecting a strong and vital personality in the class-room. The word 'charisma' has been widely used, both favourably and unfavourably, to describe the kind of impact which the teacher should accept as his ideal. The teacher is to go into the learning situation as someone who is not a transmitter of received wisdom, but an elicitor of spontaneous responses. The corollary of this is that the approach must rely very heavily on the projective personality of the individual teacher.

As I have said in the previous section, a teacher in the new style is expected to be a person who is enormously imaginatively inventive. The problem this represents for the average teacher is that he knows he is not, nor cannot be, except in rare moments, enormously imaginatively inventive. I might add that the problem for the tutor of student teachers is that there is no known way of making people enormously imaginatively inventive. Another problem is that, while a young and enthusiastic teacher may be ready to use projective personality as the consensus asks, the sheer pressure of the actual learning situation, day in day out, year in year out, leads to a moment when he realises his initial intentions have been replaced by a sense of exhaustion or even despair. Deeply embedded in the ideology of the progressive consensus, therefore, is the idea of the teacher as a dedicated and creatively inventive individual. It seems to me that, while this is a splendid ideal, if we were considering a small elite and highly professional body, it bears little useful relationship to the actual scale of a national educational system and a subject like English which requires very large numbers of individuals to practise it.

The second limitation arises from the willingness of the consensus approach to rely upon the responsiveness of the class, and the teacher's judgement of their needs, to give effective direction to the on-going pattern of work in the learning situation. How the work shapes at any one time, and where it goes, is supposed to develop from the pupils' own response to whatever is introduced as the present focus for activity. That response is elicited through the teacher's ability to read the needs of his pupils at a particular time, and create situations which meet those needs. The difficulty here is

17

that nowhere in its discussion of practice or theory does the progressive consensus offer an adequate account of what it means by 'needs'.[18] It is presumed that what we mean by pupils' needs, particularly what we might mean by the needs of those pupils often described as 'average', is self-evident to everyone. This places teachers in the difficult position of having to divine what those needs might be and then design a programme accordingly. This means that much work inspired by the progressive consensus, while excellent in the context of the single lesson or group of lessons, rapidly seems to leave pupils feeling that they are doing what they have done before, or doing the same old thing, or not getting anywhere. It is perfectly true that they may be expressing an unfortunate view of what learning is and how one goes about it, but it could be equally true that human beings are so designed that they need to feel some form of progression through a learning situation in order to satisfy themselves that learning has taken place.[19] Such a sense of progression is very often lacking, just because the response of the class is being used as the *sole* initiator and director of the activities that go on and the response itself is random rather than purposive.

The third limitation stems from the fact that the literature of the progressive consensus has yet to develop an adequate public language for the discussion of its theories and practice. In particular, much of the writing concerned seems to avoid deliberately the discussion of principles, or to discuss them non-explicitly.[20] The literature relies heavily on the brilliant, or charismatically gifted, teacher's anecdotal account of his own practice to exemplify the approach. This state of affairs seems to have generated two principal effects which hinder the more rapid adoption of the approach. First, the experience of the many able teachers who have done most to develop it is not available to the beginner in the subject in a form in which he can effectively make use of it. The literature in question makes it very difficult for him to grasp the practicalities of the practice which it is advocating, because the literature does not make use of evidence to exemplify what it theorises about. The literature is not sufficiently cool, rational and controlled in its discussion of practical problems. In much of it, there is a messianic note which leads to the use of a way of writing, a style of address to the reader, which seems to be encouraging him to 'join a movement' rather than develop a professional command of a particular approach to his work in the class-room.[21] Consequently, public debate about the

18

consensus tends to be carried on in terms of conflicting personal styles of teaching rather than alternative approaches to particular aspects of work in English which have, as their corollary, different practical realisations for pupils and teachers.

The fourth limitation is best revealed by considering the particular problems of Heads of Department. One thing that the progressive consensus makes exceedingly difficult is the ordering of a plan of work over a long period of time, whether in terms of the individual pupil, the class, or the department. It is not easy to say what the relationship between a particular piece of work done in the classroom and any explicitly stated aims and objectives in a syllabus might be. This means that a syllabus, or a plan of work for a whole department, or an outline of what the department would expect to provide during a pupil's life in the school, is virtually impossible to put down on paper except in terms so loose as to offer very little real guidance to the individual teacher, or anyone else who wants to know what is going on in the time pupils spend with the English Department. Now it is perfectly true that there is a very vocal group among those that are the strongest advocates of the progressive consensus who say that this is precisely its greatest virtue; that things like syllabuses and so on are in fact the prevention of learning; and that this is a major piece of evidence in favour of the idea that English teachers are in the vanguard of those who would rewrite the whole curriculum in terms of the individual needs of the individual learner.[22] This may or may not be a tenable position, but it seems to me to ignore the fact that in this country at the present time a very large number of teachers of English *do* have to give an account of their work to those 'put in authority over them', and do have to say explicitly what pupils will be expected to do in the course of their time with the Department.

The local effect of this limitation in the consensus approach seems to me to have produced two particular results. Many teachers, particularly young teachers who have come from Colleges of Education where the progressive consensus has been very strongly advocated, focus almost wholly upon 'the one good lesson' and do not pretend to have a strategy beyond it. In one sense, their whole approach to the job is one of 'happy chance'. What happens when the chance is unhappy is not widely discussed, except amongst other subject teachers within the profession and by the public outside, who

19

simply do not understand what is going on. The less extreme of those who implicitly reject the need for anything like structure, or an explicit direction to work in English, however, argue that activities should merely be pursued for their own sake. Activities are chosen in relation to the teacher's overall aims as an educator and the connection between activities and aims is taken to be self-evident. Much of the discussion of English in the Plowden Report was conducted along these lines. One major effect of the progressive consensus has been the strengthening of the already widely held view that there *are* activities that are 'self-evidently' valuable, and that discussion as to whether or not a particular activity is meaningful is merely theoretical and a complete waste of time for the practical teacher.

The fifth and final limitation is a specifically linguistic one. A great deal that is best in the consensus approach has concerned itself with ways and means of encouraging pupils to talk and write imaginatively.[23] In this sense, the consensus has brought about a very marked shift in focus within English teaching, away from the explicit study of literature in a literary critical sense and towards a much broader concern with language and imaginative experience. Language nevertheless has remained in an anomalous position. Though all the changes which follow from the adoption of this approach make enormous demands upon the linguistic competence of both teachers and taught, there has been little public discussion of why this should be so, what precisely creates these demands, and how they might be met and prepared for.[24] Nor has there been an adequate realisation of the degree to which the underlying bias in the progressive consensus approach towards a greater and greater concern with how we use language to live is properly and necessarily a linguistic question, and consequently demands of the teacher a distinctively linguistic perspective on language. In particular, rather than clarifying the question of competence, the consensus so far has only succeeded in making it more confused than ever it was before, because of the particular emphasis on what is generally known as 'creative writing' which lies at the centre of the class-room practice most closely identified with the approach.

Let me now try to draw this section together by singling out five particular consequences which appear to follow from the limitations in the consensus approach which I have outlined.

20

(1) Many experienced teachers, by no means fixed in their positions or attitudes, are very uneasy about what they understand by the consensus, because it seems to them that what they are being asked to do is to remove all notion of order from their class-rooms. While this is almost certainly not the case, it is important to realise the degree to which this represents the popular understanding of the direction in which English teaching is supposed to be going.

(2) Many other teachers do see the value of the principles of the consensus as they understand them, but find it exceedingly difficult to relate them to their own capabilities as individuals and as teachers. As one teacher said to me bitterly, 'I agree with it all, but what do you *do* if you're not a three-star charismatic wonder-kid?' In particular, they regard the necessary changes in the relationship between teacher and pupil as beyond their reach, because they do not see how to initiate them; nor do they see how they could retain an appropriate social control within the learning situation once this new relationship was in being. To put it technically, their dilemma is that they do not see how to retain the social control they believe essential to the class-room situation, once the social distance has been narrowed sufficiently for them to take up effectively the roles of consultant and participant.

(3) Many new teachers see an enormous credibility gap between the view of English offered to them in the course of their training, a view very largely derived from the consensus approach, and the realities of the class-room situation as they come to know them. As a consequence, many of them try the approach, as they have been encouraged to do, and run into real difficulty; cynicism or indifference from the people around them in the staff-room, or even the active hostility of older and established members of staff. Some lose heart and often go out of teaching. Others retreat to the only place where they know they are free to develop their view of English, the College of Education. Others realise very rapidly that the consensus approach will not work in the situations in which they find themselves and, in default of any alternative, turn to the way in which they themselves were taught at school in order to find a model for their own practice. As the model they recall is very often the way that they were taught in their own sixth forms, and as they are seldom teaching pupils at all

like themselves when they were at school, the results are seldom fortunate.

(4) Other subject teachers see the English Department abdicate what they regard as one of its major functions, the provision of a basic competence in written English. In many cases, they also see it at the same time arrogate to itself areas of concern for which its members appear to have no special qualifications at all. While actual instances of this are perhaps few, the popular understanding of the consensus within the profession as a whole is quite unduly influenced by the writings and activities of a few of the most vociferous advocates of the idea that English has all the answers to everybody's problems within the curriculum. Perhaps the root of this disaffection amongst other teachers is the sense that the English Department is seen to be creating a situation in its own work that affects the whole pattern of learning within the school. Once one body of teachers sets up a new pattern of relationships between teacher and pupil, it is unlikely that the effects of this can be contained within one area of the curriculum. The strongest of the advocates of the progressive consensus would point to this as one of its chief virtues, but again I would point to the realities of the situation, the fact that the majority of individuals in the profession are not in any sense revolutionary and do not wish to change society through changing the social structure of the school. It is these people whom the average teacher of English has to work with, and it is the criticism of these people that he has to answer, if he wants to be able to go on doing the things that he most wants to do.

(5) It is unfortunate that the public discussion of English teaching, as it has been conducted over the last few years, has frequently been acrimonious, a matter of taking stands, of advocating the 'one true way', of encouraging discipleship rather than a cool and rational assessment of the virtues and defects of any one particular approach or aspect of practice. It is the tone of this public discussion which seems to me to have created a climate of opinion within the profession as a whole that makes it very much more difficult for the ordinary teacher in the average school situation to try to make use of what is valuable in the progressive consensus.[25] Behind the aggressive radicalism of this public discussion, there is a holistic attitude towards the progressive consensus which does

nothing but harm, because it puts at risk the very people who ultimately have to make the consensus work in terms of real activities with actual pupils, the average teacher of English in the average secondary school.

Two Language as a focus for work in 'English'

1 Current attitudes to language in the profession

The outline of the progressive consensus and its limitations that I have given emphasises the degree to which the development of the consensus has brought about a situation in which the English teacher is increasingly asked to focus upon language, its function in the lives of his pupils and its place in his work. Perhaps the most eloquent way of pointing to the truth of this state of affairs is to consider the difference between the two international conferences in the teaching of English which have been organised by the National Association of Teachers of English in conjunction with the National Council of Teachers of English of the United States. At Dartmouth, in 1965, the question was, 'Should there be a place for language?'; in 1971, at York, the question had become, 'How should we handle language in the English classroom?'[26] The paradox remains, however, that, although the consensus approach places increasing emphasis upon language, and although the change in the relationship between teacher and pupil put a quite special emphasis on both their abilities to find new ways of using language for learning, there remains in the public discussion of the practice of English teaching a curious diffidence about the place of language. Like the member of the wedding, it is always present, but somehow no one is ever quite prepared to ask it to be the bride. Except in one or two particular places, discussion focuses on language as something other than language: as the way in which pupils write about experience; or as the means by which they can develop social relationships; or as the means by which they can acquire a powerful critique of contemporary society.[27] What has been conspicuously lacking in the discussion is any broad agreement that there needs to be a specifically *linguistic* perspective on the way in which language is used for both living and learning, by both teachers and pupils; and that this perspective is relevant to the development of a necessary explicitness in the discussion of practice, an explicitness without which the progressive consensus is unlikely to become the accepted approach of the majority of teachers of English.

As I have suggested, a linguistic perspective on language in the English class would focus attention on two distinct aspects of the consensus approach. On the one hand, such a perspective would underline the degree to which the relevant changes in practice demand of both teachers and pupils the acquisition of new ways of speaking. Furthermore, it would stress the fact that new ways of speaking do not just 'happen'. If we design materials to further the spread of this approach, we must build into those materials elements which will help teachers and pupils create the conditions in which it is possible for them to acquire the new ways of speaking that their changed relationship requires. One of the key features of *Language in Use* is that it provides ways of setting up situations in the class-room that are expressly interactional for teachers and pupils, teacher with pupil, and pupil with pupil. In other words, a linguistic per-spective would draw attention to the fact that what is implicit in the consensus approach is a desire to increase the pupil's awareness of how he uses language to live. There can be many opinions about how particular practice would increase that awareness for particular pupils, but a linguistic perspective would underline the need to make this focus *explicit*. This does not mean the production of a linguistic 'content', or examinable 'subject matter', for English. An analytical and descriptive approach to the study of language, which would correspond to the kind of content that exists in other areas of the curriculum, raises a quite separate issue and one with which this book does not need to concern itself.

There is no doubt in my mind that the effective development of the progressive consensus approach is hindered by its lack of a properly linguistic perspective on language. One major consequence of this lack is the persistence of certain widespread assumptions about lan-guage and the place of work specifically focused upon the mother tongue in the overall pattern of activities English teachers set up in their class-rooms. I would like to look now at a number of these assumptions, because they seem to me to be responsible for a set of attitudes the prevalence of which makes a new focus upon language less easy to adopt than the facts of the situation might warrant. Perhaps the very success of the progressive consensus is one factor in their persisting, as it has overlain awareness of their presence, so that they have been able to survive unexamined in the minds of many teachers who have accepted the broad programme of the consensus approach.

The first of these assumptions is the distinction between the narrow and the broad view of what is meant by language in the context of English. The narrow view sees working with language as primarily a matter of inculcating a number of basic skills, usually enumerated as spelling, punctuation and writing correct sentences: the broad view regards whatever goes on in 'English' as effectively 'working with language'. As far as the broad view is concerned, therefore, there seems to be no need for any special emphasis upon language as language, because everything going on in the English class is furthering the ultimate objective of extending pupils' command of written and spoken English and their response to both.

The second assumption concerns the English teacher's view of the attitudes towards language work in English regularly expressed by other teachers. These attitudes involve a distinction between work with language that is intended to be a basic contribution to the development of the pupil's command of the writing system and work which is supposed to make a basic contribution to the pupil's power to articulate the logic of rational discourse.[28]

The 'writing' case argues that the English teacher is the man who must provide the basic means by which pupils can meet the writing needs of other subjects. The 'thinking' case argues that the English teacher is the man who provides pupils with the basic means for comprehending the argument of a wide range of written texts and reconstructing it in his own words. Both versions of these attitudes towards language express the belief that there is a generalised capacity in relation to language which the teacher of English can make available through his work and which pupils can then take with them to use everywhere else in the curriculum. One major consequence of these attitudes, therefore, is the widespread belief that pupils should be able to meet the particular demands of other subjects without the teachers of those subjects having to give any specific attention to the language for learning which they employ.[29] The effect on the teacher of English is to make him extremely wary of any suggestion that he has anything like a 'service' function to perform in relation to the mother tongue.

The third assumption concerns the distinction in the English teacher's mind between knowledge OF English, and knowledge ABOUT English.[30] Traditionally, he has seen this distinction in terms of the distinction between a capacity to meet the requirements of school subjects in written English and the ability to perform a number of simple analytical operations on selected pieces of text, like clause analysis, and to be able to use a classification of the parts of speech in the process. The assumption was that pupils' command of written English would develop in proportion to their ability to do well in performing such exercises. Hence many teachers believe that the only justification for imparting to pupils knowledge *about* language is its power to confer a growth in their operational knowledge *of* the language. In both cases, language is usually thought of as one narrow variety of written English suitable for use in writing formally about the subject matters of the conventional curriculum subjects.

The fourth assumption is closely associated with the third. Many teachers identify knowledge *about* language with school book grammar; school book grammar with parsing; and parsing with a kind of verbal drill necessary for teaching people how to write 'good, clear English'.[31] As drill of this kind has been shown to have no significant effect upon pupils' ability to use written English, many teachers consequently now see no further justification for giving time within their classes to 'knowledge *about* language'. This particular assumption is responsible for much of the deep distrust with which teachers of English have met any suggestion that linguistics might be relevant to work with language in English, because they have identified linguistics with knowledge *about* language.

The fifth assumption arises out of a combination of the two preceding assumptions, for together they create a climate of opinion in which there is a broad recognition amongst teachers of English that encouraging pupils to write has nothing to do with extending their knowledge about their language. Essentially, encouraging pupils to write is a matter of focusing their attention upon their own experience of the world and providing a situation in which they can write about it personally and imaginatively.[32] Out of this personal focus upon putting experience into words is expected to come a generalised capacity to use written language. It would be true to say that this is a central tenet of the progressive consensus.

The sixth assumption represents another side to the question of language in English, the idea that whatever is necessary for pupils' command of the written language can derive from a proper focus

27

on the exploration of literature. This was put most explicitly and uncompromisingly some years ago by Denys Thompson when he said:

> 'the teacher's aim is to bring to life and develop his pupil's capacity for literature. There are other aims, we know; we need not despise the bread and butter tasks of developing the power of communication, but it is one that cannot engage more than a small part of the interest and energy of a teacher and his pupil . . . plenty of good reading and teaching related to it will help writing to come, almost as a by-product.'[33]

While many teachers would want to modify the uncompromising stance of this passage, they would still accept that their central function is the teaching of literature, because that is the proper basis for educating sensibility and thereby developing appropriately critical attitudes to contemporary life and culture in their pupils. From this point of view, a focus on language can have no major part in their work.

In spite of the shift in attitude since that quotation was written, I have found in audience after audience of teachers of English through the country a very strong emotional, and often practical, adherence to the broad outline of what Thompson is saying. In particular, I have found many teachers who seem to be able to combine the mainstream attitudes of the progressive consensus approach with the kind of approach which Thompson is advocating. It is almost a matter of doing a Thompson on Mondays, Wednesdays and Fridays and doing the consensus on Tuesdays, Thursdays and Saturdays.

I have outlined these six assumptions, because it seems to me that it is some combination of these six which actually underlies the practical choices the majority of teachers of English make about what to do concerning language in their own class-rooms. Taken together, these assumptions often lead teachers of English to set up a dichotomy between the vital task of enabling pupils to make the best sense of their experience of the world and the arid and formalistic exercises of an analytical approach to 'knowledge *about* language'. In the circumstances, it is hardly surprising that the majority hold to the former, and see its ideal expression in the views of the progressive consensus, while rejecting the latter as totally irrelevant to their needs and problems.

2 'English', language and linguistics

The simplest definition of Linguistics is that it is the scientific study of language. This definition underlines the fact that it is a discipline comparable in its complexity and range of concerns with familiar disciplines like Physics and History. This is an important point, because there are teachers who have the idea that linguistics is a minor auxiliary 'service' concerned primarily with the technical problems of teaching and learning foreign languages. Linguistics, like Physics or History or Psychology, embraces many different areas of interest, and offers many different directions for enquiry and exploration. Like any other discipline that impinges upon the curriculum, therefore, there will be many aspects of Linguistics that are of little or no interest to the practising teacher and have no bearing on the needs of pupils or the problems of language in teaching and learning.

There is, however, a major difference of opinion amongst linguists at the present time as to the proper scope of their discipline. This difference of opinion involves a distinction between a *narrow* and a *broad* view of the subject matter of linguistic enquiry. The narrow view sees Linguistics as a discipline which is primarily concerned with the internal organisation of the patterns of natural languages. The emphasis is upon Linguistics as a discipline, *sui generis*. The basic models for enquiry and experiment are to be drawn from the 'hard data' matter sciences like Physics and Chemistry. Like all views of well-established disciplines from the perspective of a newly emergent one, however, the 'narrow' view of what constitutes the nature of enquiry in the matter sciences accords more with the fiction of the 'disinterested observer' than with contemporary thinking and practice in those disciplines.[34]

The *broad* view of linguistic enquiry, on the other hand, would see the discipline as essentially a social or human science. It would see Linguistics as forming a triumvirate with Psychology and Sociology at the centre of that cluster of disciplines concerned with 'the proper study of mankind'. From this point of view, studying the semantics, the grammar and the phonology of a language is only a necessary means towards a proper understanding of what part the patterns of a natural language play in the individual, cultural, and social life of the people who speak it.[35] Studying the internal organisation of language is not, therefore, a sufficient end in itself to justify the activity of the discipline. The narrow view of Linguistics is dominated by the idea that the establishment of rigorous methods of enquiry are necessary in order to justify the assumption of the honorific title of 'Science'. The broad view of Linguistics, on the other hand, is dominated by the idea that the *meaning* of the discipline must not be lost sight of through a preoccupation with a validating *method* that may not in the end be as relevant to the larger aims of linguistic enquiry as it seems. There must be at the centre of the idea of the discipline a concept of language that sees it as fundamentally a variety of human behaviour. If language is an aspect of human behaviour, then its proper study cannot be considered apart from the human context that creates it and is in turn shaped by it.

At first sight, this distinction might seem to matter only to those who were themselves involved within the discipline. However, the distinction between a narrow and a broad view of Linguistics is vital for teachers, because many of them have only come across the narrow view and a not very prepossessing version of it. What they have met is a particular form of the structural analysis of the grammar of English, an analysis which would not be acceptable to contemporary linguists, because it does little more than list the surface patterns of the grammar in what is ultimately a not very illuminating fashion.[36] It is not surprising, therefore, that they cannot see how this might be meaningful to their practice or to their pupils' needs and interests. Consequently, these teachers reject the idea that Linguistics can have any relevance to them at all. Whatever has happened in recent years to modify the prevalence of this view, my experience with audiences in all parts of the country suggests that by and large it is still predominant amongst ordinary teachers of English and lecturers in College of Education Departments of English.

The whole situation is complicated by the underlying assumption, by no means confined to teachers of English, that what is useful to a teacher is necessarily what is teachable. Consequently, the argument

30

about the value or otherwise of Linguistics to the teacher of English has often been conducted in terms of its desirability or otherwise as a source of subject content for the English class. As I have said elsewhere this is a quite different matter to the one with which I am here concerned. If an 'O' Level General Linguistics is wanted to put alongside the existing 'O' Level Physics and 'O' Level Domestic Science this is an issue that has to be discussed in its own terms.[37] It has nothing to do with the much more important question as to whether or not Linguistics has something so important to say about the nature and function of language, and the way in which human beings use it to live and to learn, that no teacher can afford to ignore it.

Nor does this question of the relevance of Linguistics as a source of teachable content have anything to do with the other important question as to whether or not pupils should be encouraged to explore their own language in order to develop their awareness of its nature and function, the part that it plays in shaping them and their lives. *Language in Use* has been developed in order to show that it is possible to pursue growth of awareness as an objective without creating a Linguistics subject content for the English class. It is one way of arranging for the insights of Linguistics to be related to the particular needs of pupils in class-rooms without their being converted into a 'body of facts', with all that that means in terms of a demand for the teacher to make use of explicit informational teaching and a demand for the pupil to master both a meta-language and a technique of analysis in order to succeed.

3   Linguistics, language study and 'Language in Use'

I have suggested that a linguistic perspective on language would alert us to aspects of its nature and function that have been obscured by our habitual way of looking at language as teachers of English. In particular, it would focus attention upon the uniqueness of language as a subject for exploration in the class-room. Certainly, as far as the secondary school curriculum is concerned, language is unique, because the vast majority of secondary pupils are what linguists call 'competent native speakers'. That is to say, they have grown up in a particular family and a particular community, and have learnt how to use language to relate themselves to the world and to others in the process.[38] In their ordinary day-to-day activities outside school, therefore, pupils effectively use language to live. In this sense, when a teacher is dealing with language in the classroom, he is handling a 'subject' that his pupils have mastered in their own terms to such an extent that they already 'know' more than he will ever be able to teach them. That he may in many cases consider his pupils totally inadequate in the command of the language that they exhibit to him is more a comment upon the school system than a comment on pupils' operational knowledge of their own language.

If we accept that pupils in secondary schools are indeed competent speakers of a native language, as the linguist understands this term, then we have to take account of the fact when we set out to develop an approach to language for the English class. Let me now look at three particular consequences that follow from this position:

(1) whatever deficiencies appear in pupils' command of the spoken and written language in the context of the school situation, every pupil does have an operational knowledge of his own language sufficient for those situations with which he is experientially familiar.

As a product of acquiring this operational knowledge, moreover, a pupil will have developed a range of intuitions about how people use language, what they use it for, what kinds of language he can use, and, more importantly, what kinds he cannot.[39]

(2) Pupils have also acquired, as members of a family and of a community, assumptions about language and attitudes to its use.[40] These assumptions and attitudes the pupil does not question, because he has acquired them as a product of cultural learning, therefore they seem to him 'obvious', or 'not worth thinking about', or 'common sense', or 'what everybody thinks'.

(3) The pupil's school experience, both primary and secondary, will have added both to his intuitions about language and his stock of assumptions and attitudes concerning its nature and function. This experience will have given him a radically different perspective on language and its use, the perspective of the demands of formal learning within the subject-centred curriculum. For the majority of pupils, this experience will

have opened a vast gap between what they understand by, and can do with, language as members of their own community, and what is demanded of them in the school context. For these pupils, therefore, what they understand intuitively as using language for living, and what they understand explicitly as using language for learning, come to bear no significant relationship to each other.

It seems to me that a constructive approach to language in English must take these features into account, because they show unambiguously that what the teacher has to work with, the content of any lessons that focus upon language, is already known to his pupils; it is provided by the knowledge of the language and its use that they bring with them into the class-room. What they do not necessarily know is how to make use of that knowledge when they are faced with social situations outside the range of their experience, or when they are faced with the linguistic demands of formal learning situations. If their basic problem is not knowing how to use the knowledge that they have in situations which are unfamiliar to them, then we are unlikely to help them if we set out by assuming that their problem is a basic ignorance of the language.

Not only does the pupil stand in this unique relationship to language, however, but so also does the teacher. All of the three factors I have outlined apply as much to the teacher as they do to the pupil. Moreover, they apply to *all* teachers, not just teachers of English. There are, however, two additional factors that we have to take into account if we are primarily concerned with the teacher of English:

(1) His formal education as a teacher of English is likely to have reinforced some of his basic attitudes and assumptions about language and its use. In particular, he is likely to have a very strong idea of the primacy of the written mode over the spoken; of the viability of a single absolute standard of 'good English'; and the unique value which is believed to attach to the language of literary texts.

(2) The intellectual world of the majority of teachers of English is powerfully shaped by the fact that their basic intellectual experience has been the literary critical study of literary texts. Even now, that experience rarely contains any explicit focus

33

on the nature and function of language from a linguistic point of view.[41]

Taking these two points together, it is not unfair to say that the average teacher of English is ill prepared to assess the needs of his pupils in the area of language. It is difficult for him to examine, critically and objectively, the source and validity of his own basic assumptions about language, his attitudes towards its use, and his understanding of how an already competent native speaker can extend his command of his own language.

The particular interests, and the methods, of the scientific study of language preclude Linguistics from offering *directly* the help which teachers need. What is required, therefore, is a way of mediating between the insights of Linguistics and the linguistic needs of teachers and pupils: a way of shaping a linguistic perspective specifically focused upon the problems of language in teaching and learning. It is to this process of mediating between the powerful insights into language derivable from its linguistic study and the practical problems of language in an educational context that I have given the name of Language Study. Language Study is not, therefore, the name for a new 'subject':[42] it is the go-between that relates a coherent, ordered and explicit view of the nature and function of language to a coherent and explicit view of language in relation to learning. The key figure in this relationship, as far as the school context is concerned, is the one teacher in the school who is acknowledged to have a direct responsibility for the mother tongue, the teacher of English.

We come, therefore, to *Language in Use*. *Language in Use* is one attempt to give concrete expression to the idea of Language Study as it affects the day-to-day practice of teachers in their own classrooms. Its design relates an explicit theory of language to concrete proposals for activities and procedures in such a way that what pupils are asked to do is relatable to what we know about the nature and function of language. Moreover, the design of *Language in Use* allows pupils to pursue their work with language unaffected by the fact that what they do find out can be related to a linguistic perspective on language.

Language in Use is, therefore, a design for developing pupils' intuitions about their use of language, both written and spoken, not a programme for transmitting a body of explicit linguistic knowledge about language. At the same time, it does offer the teacher the possibility of developing a linguistic perspective on language for himself in the process of developing his pupils' awareness of how they use language to live and their competence in doing so.

Three   The design of *Language in Use*

1   An outline of the design

I have already suggested that curriculum research and development ought to relate to the context of the 'here and now' as it appears to the teacher in the class-room. This was why it was necessary to formulate a clear conception of current attitudes towards work with the mother tongue in English, in particular a clear conception of the ideas of the progressive consensus, as a first step towards the development of a new focus for language in English. At the same time, good practice, as it is here and now, is not the only factor to be taken into account: unless care is taken to build into the design the means by which the teacher can himself review its continuing relevance to his needs, all that happens is that the good practice of one moment in time is turned into the 'received view' of the next decade.

In order to ensure that his design is properly open to continuous revision when it is tested against the reality of innumerable particular learning situations, the curriculum developer must provide an explicit theory for his design. The theory must come from outside the educational context, so that the task for the curriculum developer is to relate the theory to a particular set of situations within that context. The theory must be there in order to validate the conceptual basis for his design, but the design must be tested against the relevant educational context in order to validate its pedagogic basis in terms of its effectiveness when used in actual learning situations.

Applying this idea to *Language in Use*, we can say that its conceptual basis is provided by the linguistic perspective which informs its design, a linguistic perspective that expresses a particular theory about the nature and function of language in the lives of individual men and the societies that they make. This theory is validated by reference to what Linguistics and the other Social Sciences have to say about the states of affairs in which men use language to live. The pedagogic basis for the design, however, is derived from an assessment of problems and practice in the teaching of English in Britain at the present time, seen in relation to the language needs of teachers and learners. In the following account of the design of

36

Language in Use, these two informing perspectives, the linguistic and the educational, should be seen as the joint foundation for what has been done.

I have made use of sub-headings for ease and convenience of reference in this account of the design.

The idea of the 'unit'

The key feature of the design is the *unit* (see Appendix), a plan for a sequence of lessons, occupying notionally between an hour and a half and four hours of actual class time. The unit is a plan, not a set of instructions. It has a topic, an aspect of language in use like 'Small talk', or 'Interviews', or 'Fact or fiction', related to a larger theme like 'Language and Experience' or 'Language and Social Relationships'. The text sets out a series of suggestions which are general, but concrete. It is up to the teacher to turn them into an actual sequence of events in the class-room. The unit is a means of organising thoughts about what to teach and how to teach it: it is not a substitute for the hard job of deciding what will fit the needs of a particular class at a particular point in time.[43]

There are two faces to the unit: the enquiry and the procedure. The unit outlines a way of exploring a facet of language in use. The raw material is pupils' own experience of using language, while the effective content is the growth in understanding of that experience which results from pursuing the enquiry. At the same time, the unit suggests activities and procedures for pursuing the enquiry. Activities include such things as the writing of scripts for acting or speaking; the writing of short stories or poems; the preparation of reports and findings; enacting, both scripted and improvised; the making of programmes for recording; and the use of fieldwork. Fieldwork might include the investigation of an aspect of language in use in the high street, like notices; or people's attitudes towards different ways of using language; or people's ideas about slang. Procedures focus upon work in groups of different sizes and the provision of many face-to-face situations in which pupils plan and carry out their own work tasks. These include such things as reporting back by the individual to the group, or by the group to the whole class; comment and evaluation of the work done by the pupils themselves; and contact with adults, both inside and outside school, through the use of the questionnaires.

The framework of Language in Use

The units are not simply heaped together, however; they are organised into themes. In turn, these themes are organised into three divisions. Moreover, this arrangement is not merely a matter of providing ease of reference to the units, it is the concrete expression of the linguistic perspective that underlies the whole design. Each division represents one of the three faces of language; its internal organisation; its use by the individual to order, classify and interpret his experience of the world; and the individual's use of it to initiate, maintain and control relationships with others.[44]

Part I, Language: its nature and function, embraces four themes. The first two are concerned with the use of language to convey information and to convey expression, respectively; the third explores the relationship between speech and writing; and the fourth focuses upon the patterns of the language itself.

Part II, Language and individual man, contains three themes, concerned with the way in which all our experience is modified by the fact that we have language. The first theme explores the way in which the patterns of our language affect us unconsciously; the second explores the patterns that carry the attitudes and values of the community to which we belong; and the third the way in which we can deliberately manipulate language to express our understanding of our experience.

Part III, Language and social man, also contains three themes. They are concerned with the way in which the possession of language enables us to create the very complex patterns of relationships that go to make up human society. The first theme explores the way in which we are able to use language to form individual relationships: the second theme takes one step back, and asks pupils to look at the way in which language enables us to form social groups of all shapes and sizes, maintain them over a period of time and give to them a recognisable identity: the third theme takes one more step back and asks pupils to consider how language functions as a major element in articulating the life of schools, factories, offices and communities.

This framework enables teachers to choose any piece of work from the unit store in the knowledge that they can, if they wish, relate it to an explicit theory of what language is and how it functions. The experience of the field trials showed that teachers acquire an understanding of the underlying theory simply through their practical class-room use of the units and that they particularly value the units, because they make this acquisition possible. The trials also gave evidence of the units' power to modify teachers' attitudes towards language and its use and to encourage them to take a closer look at what a linguistic perspective towards language might have to offer them.

Language in Use *in the class-room*
As the foregoing suggests, units can be used individually, or put together to form a sequence. The volume can be seen as a storehouse of ideas and a compendium of good practice. The independence of the individual unit enables a teacher to choose from the store as he wishes to match the changing pattern of needs in his classes, and to try out what they offer a little at a time, so that he does not commit himself to a vast body of work on trust.

If, however, a teacher wishes to build up a sequence of units to meet particular needs, the framework, and the theory that informs it, are there to assist him with his planning. For instance, he could plan a sequence that would help fifteen-year-olds face up to the difficulties of the adult world of work by selecting units that explore language and relationships: or he could select units which focus upon particular aspects of using written language to handle information so as to help pupils develop their command over the kind of language for learning expected of them in our secondary system.[45]

The question of age and ability
The selection of units raises the question of age and ability. Individual units, such as 'Playing many parts' and 'Social talk' have been used with classes at every age from 10+ to 18+ and across a range of ability that stretches from fourth-year leavers to postgraduate student teachers.

There are four basic factors that have made it possible for the units to be freed from a specific tie to age and ability:

    (1) They are written for the teacher and not the pupil, con-

sequently the language of the text does not have to take into account pupils as an audience.

(2) They are general, but concrete: they propose topics, give precise outlines for patterns of work, and suggest what can be done through giving examples, but *they do not specify in detail pupils' actual work or teaching procedures from moment to moment.* The teacher himself must 'realise' the actual lessons by interpreting the unit he has chosen according to the needs and abilities and interests of his own class.

(3) Because the teacher himself determines the actual details of the lesson, it is the teacher who decides upon the degree of explicitness about the work that is required of the pupil. It is the level of explicitness required of pupils, the spoken or written comment on their work that is expected of them, that is the crucial factor in determining the level of 'difficulty' of a particular pattern of work.

(4) The raw material of the units is provided by the pupils' own knowledge of how to use language to live.

This means that a unit can be used more than once with the same pupils during their passage through the school, because their experience of the world will be very different at fifteen from what it was at thirteen or eleven.

What the design of *Language in Use* does, therefore, is to provide a way of working with pupils' own knowledge of their language towards the dual objectives of awareness and competence without sacrificing the flexibility, range of concerns, or continuous creativity that characterise the virtues of the progressive consensus approach. At the same time, the unit concept, the ordering provided by the themes and their grouping, and the recommendations concerning activities and procedures, meet some of its more serious limitations in terms of actual class-room practice. Above all, it puts in the hands of ordinary teachers a way of thinking through their work with language that relates it firmly to a linguistic perspective on language and its use. I have written elsewhere concerning the theory of language upon which the *conceptual* design of *Language in Use* rests,[46] but the essence of the theory is contained in the following two quotations:

'Language intervenes between man and nature acting upon him internally and externally' (Wilhelm von Humbolt).

'The object of linguistic analysis is to make statements of meaning so that we may see how we use language to live' (J. R. Firth).

Taken together, these two quotations suggest that a focus upon language in the context of teaching and learning requires a theory of language which is neither a psychological, nor a social, nor a linguistic theory, but one which shows the essential interrelationship between these three aspects of man as a language user. For teachers, a theory of language adequate to their needs must take its point of departure from the part played by language in defining the *humanness* of human beings. It must focus upon the way in which individual human beings use language to define their experience of the world and thus define themselves as individual sentient selves; upon the way that they use language to relate to each other and thus create both societies and cultures; upon the way that language acts as the major means for transmitting, and therefore perpetuating, the attitudes and values of a society or a culture; and upon the internal organisation of this thing we call 'language' that we use in such diverse ways. If there is a uniqueness about man, then it resides in his capacity to language: and if this is the case, then there can be no more important part of a teacher's approach to his task than the perspective on language which informs it. Without an adequate theory of language, this is unlikely to meet either his own or his pupils' needs as beings uniquely defined by their capacity to use language to live and to learn.

2 Educational objectives

There are two major educational objectives for *Language in Use*. The first is an increased awareness of the nature and function of language for the pupil and the teacher: the second is an extension of the pupil's competence, his 'command of a language',[47] both spoken and written. From the teacher's point of view, his use of *Language in Use* brings him into contact with the linguistic perspective on language that informs it. He comes to see that some of the attitudes and assumptions in his own view of language need to be modified in the light of this new linguistic perspective. The response of very many teachers during the course of the field trials of *Language in Use* suggests that this objective is viable, because the material does not make a change of perspective a necessary precondition for using it in the class-room.

The use of the units also has an effect upon the teacher's own command of the language, because they allow him to come to terms with the demands of his changing professional role. The units create a situation in the class-room which encourages teachers to attempt the kind of relationship between teacher and pupil advocated by the progressive consensus. The framework of the unit enables him to see that he and the class have some idea of where they are going and what they are trying to do. Consequently, he can afford to focus his own attention, and the attention of his pupils, on the very difficult business of learning how to language and enact a new style of relationship: how to bring about what Goffman would call a new 'working consensus'.[48]

Let us now look at the first of these two objectives, awareness. Awareness is not a vague notion: it refers to the progressively greater understanding of some aspect of experience that is likely to flow from a conscious exploration of that experience. Awareness is a function of our ability to 'read' a social situation or a pattern of linguistic behaviour. Its basis lies in our ability to build up the necessary schemata as a consequence of our heuristic encounter with the relevant experience.[49] Growth of awareness results from our capacity to connect what is new with what is given in our mental universe: that is to say, growth of awareness results from our being able to relate the newness that we meet in our encounters with the world to something with which we are already familiar.[50] Clearly, I am not suggesting that this is necessarily a deliberate and analytical activity. Growth of awareness is, therefore, the development of a capacity to make use of what is new, once it has been met, because we can relate it to representations of states of affairs that are known to us. It is akin to what Jerome Bruner calls 'power to operate'.[51] We can say that we have 'power to operate' when we are able to make sense of our encounters with continuously new aspects of reality in terms of a reality that is already meaningful to us.

Let me illustrate this idea of awareness by pointing to two distinct levels at which it can function for the individual. The first of these levels I call 'insight' and the second 'perspective'. Insight comes at the point where an individual finds himself reflecting on an aspect of his experience and is able to say 'Well, I never thought that mattered to me'; or, 'I thought that was obvious, but it isn't'; or, 'I didn't think that was worth thinking about.' In this sense, it is
42

a crucial step in the development of Self. It is the moment at which the individual sees that he is free to comment upon an aspect of his experience which, up to that point, he had so taken for granted that he had scarcely been aware of its existence. The aspects of experience of which he becomes aware in this way are very frequently those that derive from the process of cultural learning. In particular, they are likely to involve those aspects of experience which are mediated through language, because language is so intimate a possession that the majority of speakers do not see it as having an existence apart from their use of it. Consequently, they do not see how it can shape and mould their understanding of themselves and the world.

The second level of awareness, perspective, is the logical and experiential extension of the first. Perspective is the ability so to distance oneself from something very familiar, even commonplace, that one can see its full significance as a dominant feature in one's own experience of the world. It is the individual's ability to say, initially, 'That's how it affects me, is it?' The next step comes at the moment when the individual is able to go on and say, 'Therefore, *that's* what it means in the lives of those I know and the society we all live in.' The final step comes when an individual can stand far enough back from his experience to be able to say, 'That's what it must mean then in the life of man. If it were not as it is, then we as a species would be different and our whole world would be different.' So perspective is the capacity to see those aspects of social and cultural reality to which we give abstract titles like language, or education, or religion, or law, not merely in terms of one's own life and how it might affect one's own individual actions, but in terms of its significance in the lives of all men and the societies that they inhabit.

The essential 'power to operate' that perspective confers, therefore, is the power to review one's own experience of the world, the events in which one is involved, the interaction one enters into, and the things to which one attaches meaning, as though all these things were happening to someone else. This concept of perspective is very close to the idea of reflexiveness as it was developed in the writings of George H. Mead.

'The evolutionary appearance of mind or intelligence takes place when the whole social process of experience and behaviour is brought within the experience of any one of the separate individuals implicated therein, and when the individual's adjustment to the process is modified and refined by the awareness or consciousness which he thus has of it. It is by means of reflexiveness—the turning-back of the experience of the individual upon himself—that the whole social process is thus brought into the experience of the individuals involved in it; it is by such means, which enable the individual to take the attitude of the other towards himself, that the individual is able consciously to adjust himself to that process, and to modify the resultant of that process in any given social act in terms of his adjustment to it. Reflexiveness, then, is the essential condition, within the social process, for the development of mind.'[52]

Growth of awareness, then, is comparable to the growth of this capacity for reflexiveness. In the context of *Language in Use*, its function as an educational objective is to suggest that we must put pupils and teachers in a position to see the way in which language processes their experience of the world and places a grid between their perception and their interpretation of it. A properly developed reflexiveness towards language would enable the individual, pupil or teacher, to see how he is himself 'made in and through language':[53] and how the society he inhabits, and the culture which informs it, are themselves products of the language which their makers speak.[54]

Growth of awareness, therefore, is quite distinct from the ability to talk about the grammatical or phonological patterns of a natural language, explicitly and analytically, using the technical language of linguistics. Growth of awareness is certainly growth of knowledge *about* one's own language, and about language in relation to the lives of individuals and societies, but it is knowledge which the individual is initially free to express in terms which he himself chooses. Moreover, this awareness derives from the individual's own knowledge *of* the language, because it is a process involving his becoming reflexive towards his own intuitions about its nature and use. Growth of awareness, however, may be carried to the point at which there is a desire to express the knowledge that results in terms which are properly public and therefore fully accessible to others. It is at this point that the individual is ready to see the potential offered him by the language of linguistic enquiry. The important point about *Language in Use*, however, is that a desire to know what linguistics has to say about language is the *product* of the explorations it instigates, not a *precondition for entering upon them.*

Let us now turn to the second of our objectives, competence. The idea of competence, the individual's command of a language, is a complex and difficult topic. It refers to the individual's total capacity to language, his ability to meet the linguistic demands of using language to live and language to learn. Growth of competence as an educational objective, therefore, must involve both spoken and written language; and it must involve a focus upon these which extends beyond the immediate local needs of a formal learning situation. Competence is a complex idea, because it embraces both the ability to language, the ability to translate 'meaning potential' into meaningful text,[55] spoken or written, and the ability to match text to context. Consequently, pursuit of competence as an educational objective necessitates a dual focus: upon the individual's experience in learning how to mean and upon his experience in learning how to make sense of the world.

Let us say, then, that growth of competence implies a growth in the individual's ability to find whatever language is requisite for the ever-widening range of situations in which he finds himself as he moves from childhood to full participation in the adult world. I would argue that the central responsibility for the teacher of English is to assist this process and everything that he does should in some sense be related to it. At the same time, the teacher of English, and all teachers, let it be said, have a special responsibility towards that particular growth of competence relevant to the linguistic needs of formal education, growth of command of language for learning. In this sense, the traditional idea that the teacher of English has a responsibility for his pupils' command of the language is a valid one. What remains open to question is what kind of responsibility that might be; what are its limits; and what is the parallel and inescapable responsibility of other teachers.[56] One aspect of the design of *Language in Use* is that it shows how the old adage, 'Every teacher is a teacher of English', can be given concrete and practical realisation in a set of activities and procedures which any teacher would be able to use in his class-room.[57]

I have said that when we speak about competence, we are concerned with the spoken language as much as the written. In terms of a general growth of competence in the use of language, in fact, it is necessary to stress the *operational* primacy of the spoken over the written mode. There is a complex, and as yet imperfectly understood, relationship between the two modes, but it does seem as though for practical purposes teachers do best to proceed as if growth of competence in spoken language comes before growth in the written language. Growth of competence in using spoken language, however, is as much a matter of developing a capacity to act in new situations as it is a question of learning new or different uses of the 'elements and structure'[58] of the language. Consequently, growth of competence is as much a matter of *social* learning as it is a question of *linguistic* learning. In fact, social learning and linguistic learning cannot really be separated from each other as though they were *independent* categories of human behaviour. They are properly *interdependent*, one upon the other, each one an aspect of the total situation in which human beings use language to create and maintain relationships. Correspondingly, command of written language is not merely a matter of articulating successfully the linguistic table manners that provide the popular notion of what 'correct' English ought to look like on the page, or a matter of learning a set of techniques under some such general heading as 'How to write an essay'. Competence in the written language is a question of matching what one wants to mean to a linguistic form that, in turn, matches the expectations of the audience for whom one is writing. It is not, therefore, a question of using a recognised 'good English' or 'logical English',[59] but a matter of being able to read all the factors in the context which point to the appropriateness of this variety of written English rather than that, for this subject matter, at this time, in relation to this audience.

We can say, therefore, that a native speaker's command of his language, his competence in the use of written and spoken language, embraces two distinct elements: his knowledge of the 'elements and structure' of his language and his knowledge of how to use them. In terms of competence as an educational objective, two major consequences follow from this distinction:

(1) Teachers can only read and hear the language that pupils actually use in the context of the learning situation. This is likely to be a very poor indicator of their linguistic resource, that is, their knowledge of the 'elements and structure' of the

language and their knowledge of how to use those 'elements and structure' in real situations in interaction with other human beings.

(2) Human beings can only learn *how* to use language *by* using it, and using it is as much a *social* as a *linguistic* act. If pupils have not had experience of social situations to which certain ways of speaking are relevant, we cannot argue from their inability to produce those ways that they lack the necessary resource, or infer that they could not produce those ways of speaking were they to be given experience of the situations in question. This must lead us to assert that a teacher's assessment of the linguistic competence for any individual pupil must include an assessment of how he has come to learn his language and what range of experience he has been exposed to in the process. There are two aspects of this situation which all teachers need to be aware of:

(i) How a pupil has learnt his language will have been shaped by the pattern of relationships existing in the family to which he belongs and the community to which his family belongs. Consequently, we can say, that between language and expression falls social structure.[60]

(ii) The way a pupil has learnt his language, in particular his idea of what he can use language for, will have shaped his existing capacity to enter into a greater or less diversity of relationships; and this in turn will have shaped the extent of his experience of the world.[61]

Individuals do what they think do-able; and what they think do-able is related both to what they have learnt to language and what they have learnt is languagable, given the circumstances in which they have grown up and the circumstances that shape their lives.

9 Awareness, competence and the English class

Let me now try to relate the educational objectives for *Language in Use* to the basic design of the material. The central problem for the design of *Language in Use* was the same in relation to both educational objectives: how can you set up a situation in which pupils will effectively modify an aspect of themselves as intimate as their intuitions about language and its use, and their operational command of their language? In both cases, it seemed essential to develop a design which would approach the relevant objective obliquely. All the evidence suggested that effective growth of awareness and competence could only come out of a heuristic situation: pupils had to be able to work through a relevant body of experience in their own terms, otherwise they would merely react against what was being offered.

Enquiries which the individual units recommend provide the pupil with the opportunity to explore language in an orderly way, but yet in his own terms. Through the heuristic involved, he comes to examine his own assumptions about language and modify his intuitions about it, because he explores what is already familiar to him as everyday experience. What is new to him is the idea that he should focus upon this experience and try to make sense of it. It is the *content* of the unit, therefore, which directs the pupil towards the objective of *awareness*.

In relation to competence, the units had to take into account the following three factors:

(1) Using language effectively requires the user to 'read' real situations and derive from them specifications for relevant language activity.
(2) Being able to 'mean' in real situations is a result of the capacity to derive from a knowledge of the language, therefore, text capable of meeting such specification.[62]
(3) Learning how to 'mean', therefore, is a matter of learning how to determine what is an appropriate linguistic response to the linguistic demands of real situations. It is important to see that this idea of linguistic appropriateness arises out of the nature of human interaction and is not at all akin to the idea of a universally applicable standard or norm of good usage. The idea of appropriateness underlines the need for there to be a fit or match between the meanings relevant to a situation and the linguistic realisations which the participants give to them.

It is the *activities* and *procedures* in the units which are directed towards this *competence*. They provide a framework in which a great deal of the work is carried on face-to-face. There is a continuous

48

use of specific situations calling for the exercise of many different ways of using language, both spoken and written. It is through the activities and procedures which the units recommend that *Language in Use* creates in the class-room the conditions of real situations through participation in which pupils can effectively extend their command over spoken and written language.

Thus the dual form of the unit relates our two objectives to each other. The content of the unit, the enquiry it offers and the pattern of exploration to which it leads, is directed towards the growth of awareness: while its activities and procedures, what is done in the course of that exploration, what happens in the way of talking and writing, is directed towards the growth of competence. Content and procedure, however, come together to produce a single interlocking pattern and thus offer a continuous interrelationship between pursuit of awareness and pursuit of competence.

This interrelationship is a vital aspect of the whole enterprise, because awareness has a crucial part to play in bringing about the growth of competence, while this growth of competence in turn brings about a further growth of awareness, because this growth makes it progressively more possible for pupils to language their understanding of how they use language to live and to learn. Growth of competence is encouraged by a developing growth of awareness, because growth of competence, as we have seen, is more a matter of learning *what* and *when* and *in what manner*, to language, than a question of learning more elements and structure of the language. By developing pupils' awareness of how language functions, of how it *is* used, teachers are showing them what the possibilities for languaging actually are. By setting up work in the class-room in such a way that the exploration of language is a *social* process for all those involved, he can provide the opportunities to try out and develop in real situations these newly grasped possibilities. It is the central function of the design of the unit that it provides a framework which makes the creation of such real situations a practical possibility.

As this point is so central to the whole enterprise, let me end by setting out the four basic reasons why it has been possible to design a unit for the class-room that does interrelate the objectives of awareness and competence in the desired way. Perhaps I would now go as far as to say that any approach to language work in the mother tongue which does not take into account these four points is unlikely to produce a design for materials which will achieve the objectives in question.

(1) The exercise of competence depends essentially upon an individual's capacity to read, or interpret, the real situations in which he finds himself called upon to language; and then to match his reading to his existing knowledge of the language in order to select text that is appropriate to the situation.

(2) This capacity to read a situation depends upon the sharpness with which the individual can assess the factors which bear upon an appropriate choice of text.

(3) This means that successful languaging depends upon a developed awareness of oneself as an active participant in real situations, and of the degree to which the activity of languaging itself involves a process of selecting continuously from a wide or narrow range of possibilities, wide or narrow according to the circumstances in question.[63] Clearly, however, awareness operates for the most part intuitively: that is to say, we are not *necessarily* conscious that what we are doing in a particular situation is making a whole series of decisions about what to say and how to say it. On the other hand, we are all familiar with situations where we are in fact in very conscious control of what we say.

(4) Hence the development of awareness, as I have defined it, is a necessary precondition for *effective* growth of competence, because it is our awareness that provides us with a reading for the situations in which we are required to language. It is on that reading that we base our choice of what to say and how to say it.

REFERENCES

1. The 'teacher proof' curriculum programmes of the U.S.A. provide the best examples.
2. This has been the approach adopted by several Schools Council projects in the area of 'English'.
3. cf. Hanson (1958) and Johnson Abercrombie (1960).
4. Medawar (1969), p. 59.
5. Bantock (1971).

6. Holbrook (1964) and Inglis (1969) exemplify the *non-public* stance, Britton (1970) the public.
7. Creber (1965), Inglis (1971) and Whitehead (1966).
8. Doughty (1968) (a).
9. Doughty, Pearce and Thornton (1972), Ch. 7, 'Command of a language'.
10. Doughty and Thornton (1973), Ch. 2, ii, 'Language for living and language for learning'.
11. Doughty (1968) (a), Part V.
12. Whitehead (1966), Ch. 1.
13. Ford (1965), p. 8.
14. The Black Papers, published by the *Critical Quarterly*, are a fertile source of comment of this kind.
15. Goffman (1959), p. 15.
16. Doughty, Pearce and Thornton (1972), Ch. 5, 'Language and relationships'.
17. Doughty, Pearce and Thornton (1972), p. 122.
18. Doughty and Thornton (1973), Ch. 1, iv, 'The "needs" of learners'.
19. Young (1971), pp. 603 et seq.
20. A conspicuous exception has been the 'Principles' issues of *English in Education*, Vol. 4, No. 1 (1970); Vol. 5, No. 1 (1971); Vol. 6, No. 1 (1972).
21. Doughty (1972).
22. This view was implicit in much that was said by the 'Commission 7' group at the York International Conference, 1971.
23. Dixon (1967), Creber (1965).
24. Hannan *et al.* (1971) and Britton (1970) are significant exceptions.
25. cf. Inglis (1971).
26. Booth (1971).
27. Doughty (1968) (a), pp. 60 et seq.
28. Doughty (1968) (b), p. 15.
29. Doughty, Pearce and Thornton (1972), p. 18. See also Doughty and Thornton (1973), Ch. 2, 'Cultural attitudes, language and the learning situation'.
30. Doughty, Pearce and Thornton (1972), pp. 21 et seq.
31. Doughty (1968) (b), p. 19.
32. Dixon (1967).
33. 'A reflection', in *English in Education*, ed. Brian Jackson and Denys Thompson.
34. For a contemporary perspective on the nature of scientific enquiry see Medawar (1967), especially 'Two conceptions of science' and 'Hypothesis and imagination', where Medawar's characterisation of 'the scientific method' corresponds closely to what I have suggested is the underlying perspective of the 'narrow' view of linguistics. See also Medawar (1969) and Popper (1963), especially 'On the sources of knowledge and of ignorance'.
35. Firth (1957), *Personality and Language in Society*.
36. Two good examples are provided by the writings of Charles Fries and Paul Roberts for the class-room.

37. See Professor Randolph Quirk's appendix to the Eighth Report of the Secondary Schools Examinations Council, H.M.S.O., 1964.
38. Doughty, Pearce and Thornton (1972), Ch. 3, 'The language we acquire'. See also Doughty, Peter and Anne (1974).
39. Halliday (1973), 'Relevant models of language'.
40. These attitudes and assumptions constitute the individual's 'folk-linguistic' view of language. See Doughty, Pearce and Thornton (1972), pp. 8 et seq.
41. For a discussion of the literary critical bias in the English teacher's attitude to language, see Doughty (1968) (c), especially pp. 6 et seq.
42. Doughty and Thornton (1973), Ch. 4, 'Language study: discipline or process?'
43. The references here are to the names of individual units in *Language in Use*, Doughty, Pearce and Thornton (1971).
44. The concept of the 'three faces' is developed through the ten theme introductions in *Language in Use*.
45. The idea of sequences is further developed in the section, 'Using the units', *Language in Use*, p. 265.
46. Doughty (1972), pp. 22 et seq.
47. Doughty, Pearce and Thornton (1972), p. 106.
48. Goffman (1959), p. 80.
49. For the idea of 'schemata', see Johnson Abercrombie (1960), pp. 30 et seq.
50. Bannister and Fransella (1971), p. 19.
51. Bruner (1965), pp. 53 et seq.
52. Mead (1934), p. 134.
53. Booth (1971).
54. Doughty, Peter and Anne (1974).
55. Halliday (1973), p. 72.
56. Doughty, Pearce and Thorton (1972), p. 18.
57. Doughty, Peter and Anne (forthcoming).
58. For the concept of 'elements and structure', see Doughty, Pearce and Thornton (1972), p. 110.
59. Doughty (1968) (b).
60. Bernstein (1972).
61. Doughty, Peter and Anne (1974).
62. Halliday (1973), p. 30.
63. Halliday (1973), pp. 55 et seq.

PART II

'English' in the curriculum: an examination of the objectives, aims and approaches currently revealed by the work of the English class

One   Public and professional attitudes to 'English' and their origins

'What is the English teacher really up to?' This question is a familiar one. What is it about 'English' that leads so many people, both inside and outside education, to ask this particular question, very often the *only* question about the curriculum that they do ask? The question would suggest that there is neither a popular, nor an educational, consensus about the part English should play in pupils' life at school. This uncertainty about English is amplified by the English teacher's own uncertainties about the part his subject should play in the curriculum. A major factor in the current confusion over English, however, is certainly provided by public and private misconceptions about the aims and objectives which might be properly assigned to the subject. Before I explore the English teacher's own idea of his aims and objectives, I want, therefore, to look a little more closely at the attitudes to English which exist at present amongst the rest of the teaching profession and amongst the public outside the world of school and college.

Both public and professional attitudes cover a range of questions which extend from the actual details of day-to-day practice, like the teaching of reading and writing, to much more fundamental issues, such as the validity of 'free drama', the use of 'creative writing', or the development of a critical awareness of social institutions. Let me suggest we approach this problem by distinguishing, first, between:

(1) What teachers of English believe to be their aims and objectives, together with the activities they employ.

(2) What *others* believe those aims and objectives to be; and what they believe they ought to be.

Then we can distinguish between two bodies of opinion amongst these 'others':

(i) the professional—what teachers *other than teachers of English* believe the teacher of English ought to contribute to the work of the school, college or university.
(ii) the public—the views of parents, employers, public dignitaries: all those, in fact, who feel they have a right to comment upon what they expect the teacher of English to contribute to the life of the community.

For the moment, then, let me leave on one side the English teacher's own view of his task and concentrate upon these alternative views of English, the public and the professional. Both professional and public opinion about English tends to employ one, or a combination, of three basic attitudes towards the subject; the normative, the pragmatical and the cultural. They can be expressed in terms of the kind of competence[1] that they demand of pupils, whether as learners within the local environment of the school; as students within the educational system as a whole; or as future adult members of a complex industrial society.

The normative
Pupils and school leavers should be able to write and talk in ways consonant with prevailing notions of what constitutes 'good English', 'clear speech', or 'logical thought'.[2]

The pragmatical
Pupils should be able to execute specific linguistic operations, like conveying a message by telephone, writing out a requisition, reading a textbook, writing up an experiment, or using a service schedule, in a way that satisfies the linguistic preconceptions of those who require their performance. The underlying idea is that the English teacher should be able to provide an 'all-purpose tool-kit' for doing language jobs about the school, the college, the office, the factory, the home, and the community.

The cultural
This attitude to the role of English is usually less clearly articulated
54

than either the normative or the pragmatical, but usually the implication is that all pupils should come into contact with 'our glorious heritage of literature'. A more sophisticated version of this view believes that 'literature must be kept up' or civilisation will die— 'literature' in this case being those writers to whom the speaker in question attaches particular value. There is an extreme version of this view which would seem to be suggesting that those who don't know what century Wordsworth was born in are as good as illiterate.

These three attitudes to the role of English are really expressions of a common consciousness, what 'the wisdom of the tribe' regards as English and sees as a justification for its presence in the curriculum.

Let me return for a moment to the teacher of English himself. As the three attitudes I have mentioned are part of our common consciousness, it is not surprising that they influence the view of his subject which the teacher of English himself holds, however much they may be refined in expression or detail by his close attention to their relevance for his practice in the class-room. For example, the cultural attitude to English has had an enormous influence upon work in the English class in the form given to it by the Scrutiny tradition and its advocates. This view of English has been powerfully articulated in the literature of the subject and is too well known to require comment.[3] There are two aspects to this version of the cultural attitude to English, however, which it would be useful to distinguish at this stage of the argument:

The moralistic
The study of high literature is the foundation for the development of pupils' moral sensibility. The English teacher is seen as properly, or primarily, or even exclusively, the one person in school or college who can claim responsibility for the pupil's growth of moral awareness, his ability to answer F. L. Leavis' question 'What for? What ultimately for?' Translated into class-room terms, this means that growth of sensibility necessarily involves the close consideration of personal relationships; and that this consideration is best carried on in the context of school or college through the study of what the best writers have had to say about life.[4] Consequently, the proper focus for the work of the English class must be the study of literature.

The expressive
The primary responsibilty of the teacher of English is towards the development of his pupils' response to imaginative language, whether it appears in the works of established writers, or in his own use of the language to describe his personal experience of the world.[5]

If we now take up again our basic distinction between a professional and a public view of English in the curriculum, we can see that there is one sense in which they both derive from a common source, because schools and colleges are as much a part of the community as factories, banks or offices. The question we need to ask, therefore, is the precise nature of the relationship between the views that arise within the professional world of the educational system and the views that are to be found in the society to which that educational system belongs.[6] There are four questions which we can ask about this relationship:

(1) Are professional attitudes *merely* a reflection of public attitudes, so that there is really only one body of opinion about English and the apparent differences that we can see simply reflect the minor differences of emphasis occasioned by the different needs and functions of schools and colleges, offices and factories, rather than any major differences of substance?

(2) If there is not just one body of opinion, then what is unique about professional attitudes towards English and how does that uniqueness arise?

(3) If we accept that there are attitudes towards English which only arise in the context of the educational system, are these attitudes the *whole* of professional opinion, or do they combine with attitudes that are indistinguishable from those expressed by the public at large?

(4) If we accept that professional opinion about English is made up of a combination of attitudes, some of which arise in the local context of the learning situation, and some of which exist within the life of a particular community, what then is the relationship between them, and how does this relationship affect decision-making in the class-room?

Where, then, and how, do attitudes towards English originate; and, having come into being, how are they perpetuated? The answer to this question lies in the relationship between an agency, such as a school or a college, and the society to which it belongs. What we have to focus upon is the way in which schools and colleges derive their values from the values of the society which they serve.[7]

Communities develop and maintain a 'wisdom of the tribe', a whole body of attitudes and assumptions about the world which a person acquires merely by growing up in a particular place at a particular time. As he acquires them unconsciously, he is often unaware that they *are* attitudes. He regards them as the 'obvious' or the common-sense way of looking at the world, or an aspect of it, and usually retains an uncritical stance towards his acceptance of the values they express. Obviously, this 'wisdom of the tribe' will include attitudes and assumptions about language and the use of language, and the particular values they express form a 'folk-linguistic' perspective on the nature and function of language.[8] This 'folk-linguistic' contributes a major part of what we have described as public opinion about English. As ordinary members of society, teachers will acquire 'the wisdom of their tribe' along with everyone else, consequently they will acquire the prevailing 'folk-linguistic' attitudes along with everyone else. These 'folk-linguistic' attitudes must, therefore, necessarily enter into the composition of the professional view of English.

Schools use language, and everyone who goes to school acquires attitudes and assumptions about language and the use of language from that experience. People also acquire a view of what English appears to be, both from being taught it, and being exposed to the professional view of it through their contact with the teachers of all the other subjects in the curriculum. As these subject teachers derive their basic attitudes to English from the attitudes most widely held in the community, and as their professional training has often done very little to modify those attitudes, what pupils usually meet at school, therefore, are *public attitudes to English made explicit and given the status of 'knowledge' through their occurrence in the formal context of the class-room.* Thus the majority of people derive from school a view of English that is a version of the public view. It is made explicit for them when they meet it as a set of requirements that they are expected to satisfy as users of language for learning, and is thus sanctioned by the value system of the school. So the school is the major agency through which existing public views about English are made explicit, validated, and thus maintained as part of what everybody knows they know about English.

The argument of the previous paragraphs would seem to contradict what was said earlier about there being a body of opinion concerning English which was unique to the school context. This contradiction is only apparent, however, for the uniqueness of the professional view derives from the explicitness of statement, and the context in which it is expressed, rather than in any difference in substance from the public view. What the pupil is normally faced with in any class-room is the teacher's articulated attitude to English as an ordinary educated adult member of his community. The specifically *professional* aspect of teacher's attitudes emerges only in discussion and comment with teachers of English and is not therefore available to the pupil. Any uniqueness in professional attitudes to English arises from the fact that they are circumscribed by the demands of teaching and learning. Professional opinion about English, therefore, is shaped by the fact that all teachers are necessarily consumers of a particular kind of 'communicative competence',[9] what I call 'language for learning',[10] and they look to the English Department to provide their pupils with this.

If we now look at the work of the English teacher himself in the light of this argument, we can see that much of it applies to him also. It is very often the case that the teacher of English expresses public attitudes to English, as much as any other teacher, in so far as those attitudes are concerned with the language and its use, although he does have his own specifically English view of the aspects of his work which he regards as the centre of his concerns as a teacher of English. In the minds of pupils, and therefore, in the minds of future educated adult members of the community, the English teacher's specifically English view of English seems often to remain closely bound to the context of the English class-room, and appears to have little power to modify existing public attitudes to English. The attitudes to English the individual may derive from his work in the English class-room are likely to continue to exist in his mind alongside the public view, as though belonging to a different world of 'literature' or 'poetry' or 'personal writing', or be rejected entirely as 'what we did in school' and therefore, by definition, not relevant to the 'real world' outside.[11]

58

This exploration of professional and public attitudes to English suggests that we may be able to make a statement about professional attitudes which would be a general statement about the kinds of attitudes that influence the formation of a professional view of any subject within the curriculum. There would seem to be four distinct sets of these attitudes:

(1) The teacher's attitudes to his own discipline; what a teacher regards as properly the nature and scope of his subject, that is, his perspective on that aspect of reality which is the particular focus for his chosen field of operations as a teacher.

(2) The teacher's attitudes to the teaching of his discipline; what a teacher regards as properly his day-to-day task in relation to a formal learning situation, that is, his view of 'good practice'.[12]

(3) The teacher's attitudes, as a teacher, to a discipline he considers relevant to his own activities in the class-room; a teacher's view of what English ought to provide for his use as a consumer of 'communicative competence', for instance.

(4) The teacher's attitudes to a subject in the context of school or college; what he, as an educated member of the community, thinks a subject ought, and ought not, to concern itself with in relation to purposes of formal education.

If we now look at the particular case of professional attitudes to English, in the light of this formulation, we can suggest that the formation of professional opinion about English is complicated by the unique status of English as both a curriculum subject and the name for the language through which every subject makes itself known to the learner. There are four aspects of this uniqueness which are particularly relevant in the present context:

(1) The fact that there is a very wide gap between what teachers understand by English, as a result of their formal educational experience of it, and what they feel they require from the subject in relation to their own class-room situation.

(2) The fact that teachers' views of English are, therefore, dominated by their concern for its fundamental importance as a service, as the provider of 'language for learning', while teachers of English seem to them to be most concerned with things that appear irrelevant to this service function.

(3) The fact that professional attitudes to English are really inseparable from public attitudes to English. These attitudes to the language are the product of cultural learning and therefore intuitive in operation. Consequently, they are highly resistant to examination or change.[13]

(4) The fact that attitudes to language are the expression of very complex attitudes to social and moral behaviour, so that attitudes to English often reflect a set of underlying attitudes about social order and public morality.[14]

Up to this point, I have written as though there were a consensus view of English as far as *public* attitudes are concerned; and that what is mediated through the value system of the school or college is an explicit version of these attitudes. If this is the case, then there are two further points that we have to consider.

First, we can suggest that if the major determining factor in public attitudes to English is the view of English which people acquire as a result of their own school experience, then the public view of English is likely to express a view of English appropriate to a time, not one, but two generations prior to the present. People at present in a position to formulate public attitudes are likely to have been at school themselves between fifteen and thirty years ago. They will have been taught in turn by people whose own attitudes were formed a further fifteen to thirty years prior to the time at which the teaching was taking place. So we can say that contemporary public attitudes to English are being powerfully influenced by attitudes which were current in English society during the nineteen-twenties and thirties. Given the relationship we have established between public and professional views of a subject, this time-shift in attitudes will apply equally to current professional attitudes to English. At a time when the view of his subject held by the teacher of English is undergoing rapid and radical change, the credibility gap between the public and professional view of his task, therefore, and what he himself may think of it, has grown to be excessively wide.

Secondly, I would suggest that the basic idea of a consensus view of English does need to be modified. Such a consensus certainly exists in our society, but it expresses the attitudes and linguistic predilections of one particular social group[15] within it rather than the received wisdom of the whole community. Language is one of the major means by which social groups achieve the cohesion that gives them identity and continuity,[16] that is, enables them to exist as a distinct entity within the general fabric of society. It is not surprising then that attitudes to language and its use form an important part of the values that express the group's sense of collective identity. We have already seen, however, that a public view of English is often indistinguishable from a public view of language and its use. Consequently, there is a very close tie between a public view of English and the attitudes towards language and its use which express the collective received wisdom of particular social groups.

In the context of English, the problem is that the public view of English which informs our society expresses the values of the dominant socio-economic group within it, the middle class. It is a truism that the dominant socio-economic group in a society determines the shape and content of its educational system and effectively controls the terms of access to its various levels, and the criteria for success within it.[17] Consequently, it is not surprising to find that the attitudes to English which do most to determine both public and professional views of the subject in its educational context are really an expression of what is accepted as apt or relevant or desirable for pupils to learn about English, judged according to the values of the middle class. If we consider that some 70% of the school population cannot be considered in these terms, middle class, and that the majority of teachers either come from the 30% who can, or have accepted the value system of that 30% by the time they have finished their training as teachers, then we can see that there is an enormous potential for a persistent clash of attitudes between pupil and teacher over language and its use.

Two The problem of describing the variousness of English as seen by the teacher of English

Having set out the general position regarding attitudes to English and placed the teacher of English within it, it is now time to focus upon the position of English in the curriculum as seen from the point of view of the specialist teacher of English. The most obvious point is that there is no current consensus which expresses a majority view of what English ought to be. Teachers of English are conspicuous for the fact that they seem to talk with as many voices as there are contributors to the debate. I hope to show that the position is not quite what it appears on the surface, however; and that the use of an appropriate formal approach to the problem of the variousness of English reveals the existence of very wide areas of general agreement.

The crux of the matter is the difficulty teachers of English have had in reconciling the enormous diversity of their interests and practice with any set of categories which would give some kind of generality to statements about work in English. In fact, one particular group amongst them would go so far as to say that any such reconciliation is not only impossible, but positively undesirable, as it would represent a fundamental distortion of the essential nature of the English teacher's proper task, the development of whole human beings. I would suggest that this is a council of despair, or even, perhaps, an evasion of the basic requirement that a teacher ought to know what he is doing and why he is doing it.

It is reasonable to expect that a teacher should be able to give an explicit and rational account of his practice and the principled basis from which it derives. Teaching is a process of continuous decision-making; decisions are made according to an individual's pre-existing view of the total situation in which the decision has to be made; in this sense, his particular decisions derive from a theory about the activity in question. He can operate his theory intuitively, or he can make it explicit to himself and relate his decisions to it, but what he does not have the option of doing is to dispense with a theory altogether. In so far as a teacher of English makes day-to-day decisions about what his pupils should write, what they should read, what themes they should explore, what experiences they should discuss, he is operating a theory of English teaching, a principled basis for making those decisions. His option is to keep himself ignorant of the basis of the practical decisions he makes, the effect of which is so immediate and decisive for his pupils: or try to formulate for himself why he is doing what he is doing, even if, in the process, he had to admit that one reason for doing what he was doing was to get to the end of the day without a riot, or to get his pupils through the examination.

The need then is for a *formal* model that will identify a number of basic features which affect the teacher's decision-making in learning situations; show how these combine in creating a teacher's own working 'theory of English'; and how his theory of English can be related to the multiplicity of practical decisions he reaches in the normal course of his day-to-day work in the class-room. The most important requirement of the model is that it show the components of a theory of English as discrete features, so that their nature and function can be properly considered, and yet avoid the suggestion *that anyone of those features is likely to occur in the class-room situation independently of any other*. Stated in these terms, the problem assumes a shape that will appear familiar to anyone who has been concerned with recent developments in the life sciences or social sciences. It is the problem of relating a small set of features, each one of which can be distinguished from all the others, to an indefinitely large number of combinations of those features in an indefinitely large number of individual environments. Another way of stating the position is to say that what we find in an English class-room is a unique combination of features which are themselves nevertheless likely to occur in many other English class-rooms in combinations just as unique.

My own work over the last eight years in the field of Linguistic Science has made me familiar with the formal models which contemporary linguists have developed for coping with just this situation, where it occurs in the context of the description of natural languages. In particular, I have been strongly influenced by the formal model for linguistic description developed by Professor M. A. K. Halliday.[18] It has seemed to me for some time that it had great potential for enabling us to cope with the enormous diversity of actual learning situations which occur within so individualistic a field of teaching as English. It would enable us to do proper justice to the inventiveness implied by that diversity,[19] while at the same time offering us the opportunity to achieve a proper measure of generality. In other words, we might be able to describe what teachers of English must share in common, because they *are* teachers of English; and yet preserve the sense that each individual act of teaching is a unique event.

Linguistics is still a very unfamiliar field and its conceptual world is not widely available, but this is not the place to give a detailed account of linguistic models, nor would this be appropriate to my purpose.[20] What I want to do is to present the source of the model which I am constructing, informally, so that a reader can go on to the detailed description of the model with some idea of where it has come from.

Let us consider for a moment the central problem facing the linguist when he tries to understand how language works. Using language, whether in speaking or writing, involves the continuous invention of new combinations of a common stock of elements. The newness arises from the uniqueness of each situation of speaking or writing in which the speaker finds himself: the commonness of the elements which he combines is self-evident from the fact that users of the same language can understand each other's use of it. Perhaps the following analogy may help. We could say that using language is like designing aeroplanes. Any design makes use of wings, fuselage, fins, ailerons, undercarriage, cockpit, and so on, yet we have little difficulty in distinguishing one design from another. Let us carry the analogy a little further. Planes tend to be designed for particular contexts, military or civil, and elements like gun-turrets, bomb-doors, air-to-air radar, passenger seating, are relevant for selection in one of these contexts, but not necessarily in others. Some planes show a radical design, such as swing-wing interceptors or helicopters, and thus do not reveal the 'obvious' features of the conventional aeroplane.

When I said earlier that each situation of speaking was unique, some readers may have felt uneasy. What, they might have thought, is unique about saying 'Pass the salt', or 'Good morning'? The analogy of the aeroplane may help here. Once designed, an unlimited number of planes can be produced to the same design, according to the needs of the user and so long as he has access to the design and the resources for its production. The design itself must also continue to satisfy the particular operational requirements it was originally intended to meet. A unique combination of features made the Spitfire the Spitfire, while any actual Spitfire was one occurrence of that combination. It is, however, a combination of features that no longer meet the operational requirements of an interceptor, so Spitfires are no longer built.

In describing the grammar of a language, the linguist is concerned with similar combinations of features and their relation to unique instances of them as they occur in ordinary speech and writing. One way of dealing with this situation as it occurs in natural languages is to say that any particular utterance is one instance of a particular combination of elements and the relationship between them. If I am asked a question after speaking to an audience of teachers, and say in reply, 'I teach English', I have used an utterance that is one unique occurrence of a particular combination of features, just as an actual Spitfire was a unique occurrence of that particular design. There are two aspects of this combination, however. In making the utterance, I combine pronoun, verb and noun: fuselage, wings and tailplane, as it were. In combining these linguistic elements, however, I set up relationships between them, the relationships we name when we use terms such as 'subject' and 'object', or 'tense' and 'number' and 'person'. That is to say, in making my utterances, I combine elements, common to very many utterances, and make a structure, a pattern of relationships which serves a particular purpose and may fit many utterances, but not all those that can be made out of the same elements. Drawing upon our analogy again, we can say that particular types of combinations of wings, fuselage and tailplane are a level of organisation which comes between these individual common elements and particular designs like the Spitfire. We give them names like interceptor, transport, short-haul jet, seaplane, and so on. These combinations of common elements represent a level of organisation in aircraft design that is making general statements about what planes are used for, rather than discriminating between individual designs for aeroplanes.

So we have the following situation in language. Every utterance is a unique occurrence of a particular combination of 'elements and structure'. The same set of elements, however, can be combined to

65

produce a number of distinctly different structures, and what creates the distinctness between them is not so much the presence or absence of any one element, but the nature of the pattern of relationships which is established between those that are made use of.

There is one further step to take before we can apply this model to the context of English. We can say that what has been outlined above represents a series of choices. The language provides a set of elements or features: we select from these features and combine them to make a number of structures. In a particular situation, we select our structures and produce an actual utterance that fits our needs. We can say that the words we actually speak *realise*[21] that combination of elements and structure on that particular occasion. At the same time we need to remember that there is a further question we can ask: What has led us to choose that particular combination of elements and structure on that particular occasion? The answer to this question is not to be found by looking at the elements and structure themselves. We have to consider the possibility of a further level of organisation which determines how we select our elements and structure. In linguistics, this leads us to consider a level of semantic organisation which decides what will be selected from the level of organisation represented by elements and structure, the grammar of a language.[22] This should warn us that it will not be enough to set up our model so that it can cope successfully with the diversity of activities and procedures in English. We will also want to show what affects our choice of one set of aims and procedures rather than another.

Now how does this help us to make sense of the teacher's practical problems? My prior assumption, as I have said, is that he needs to be able to see that the most important aspect of his job is the decisions he makes about what to do with his pupils. My suggestion is that a formal model of the kind I shall outline will help him to see *how* he makes these decisions, what elements and structure enter into them, and consequently how he might be able to evaluate them, or, in other words, say why he is doing what he is doing, and what a successful outcome might look like.

If we now try to relate this model to the class-room, we can begin by suggesting that the intended pattern of an actual lesson repre-

66

sents a series of choices that a particular teacher makes in relation to a particular learning situation. The area of the curriculum involved provides the teacher with a set of *objectives*. He makes his selection from these objectives and combines them in such a way as to give him a direction or focus for his work in the class-room. This focus we will call his *aim*. This aim is what guides the actual pattern of work he devises to meet the needs of the particular learning situation in question. We can say, therefore, that those activities and procedures which actually occur in the class-room are the practical *realisations* of the particular combination of *objectives* which go to form the teacher's guiding *aim* for his work.

A teacher's theory of English is, therefore, the concrete expression of particular combinations of objectives, and the aims to which these combinations give rise. In so far as the objectives are related to English as an area of the curriculum, they are shared by, or at least, available to, all other teachers of English. In so far as it is possible to derive only a limited number of combinations from them, many teachers will share aims in common, and we can predict that some particular combinations are likely to occur much more often (in particular contexts) than others. The uniqueness in each teacher's theory, however, enters at the point where he has to realise a particular combination of the elements and structure of English, its objectives and aims, in terms of an actual sequence of work in a particular learning situation. Objectives and aims give teachers of English a shared basis for a common 'theory of English', but how they use the theory in direct contact with their own classes admits of as much individual variation as language itself.

In English there has been a tendency to stress the uniqueness of each teacher's practice, so that the elements it shares in common with the practice of other teachers of English has been obscured, or actively discounted.[23] What is, in the fullest sense, unique about a learning situation is what is contingent to it: this teacher, these pupils, at this point in their progress through the school, in this class-room, at this point in the day, the week and the term, in this school, in this community. This is a quality of uniqueness that a pattern of teaching shares with a pattern of utterance. There is, however, a further quality of uniqueness that resides in the individuality that a person brings to his use of common elements and structure, be they the elements and structures of his language or

67

English. It resides, not so much in what he actually uses, but in the way that he combines the features that he selects to make meaningful relationships which are capable of expressing exactly what *he* wants to say. In particular, it resides in the weight which he gives to one possible meaning rather than any other: it resides, for the teacher, in his choice of content and theme and the activities and procedures he sees as the most appropriate realisations for them in the particular context of an actual class-room at a specific point in time.

In this discussion I have made use of the familar convention that allows a writer to speak of an individual 'choosing' and 'selecting' as though this were a deliberate and conscious activity carried on all the time with a full knowledge of what is being selected. In the context of teaching certainly this may be the case on rare occasions, but the much more familiar situation is one in which decisions of this order are made intuitively by the teacher in the act of teaching. We recognise this by implication whenever we refer to the idea of 'experience' as that quality most necessary to 'good practice', because it is through the making of innumerable practical decisions from day to day that we develop our 'theory', our own individual ideas about objectives and the combinations that they make possible. In this sense, selecting from the elements and structure of English in the course of one's practice is closely analogous to selecting from the elements and structure of English when we speak or write. In fact, there is good evidence for suggesting the similarity in the process may be substantive rather than analogous.[24]

In what follows, therefore, the stress upon what teachers of English share in common must not be read as a bid to iron out or undervalue what makes one teacher different from every other. The argument is that any teacher will best come to understand his own particular and unique interpretation of English if he can see clearly what elements and structure he has chosen from the common ground of a 'theory of English' practice, and how these combine in his work from day to day and class to class.

Three Using a formal model to chart the variousness of English practice

1 The basic categories of the model

What now follows is the outline of a formal model which would help us to cope with the diversity of views about English and the variousness of English practice as it exists at the present time. The focus is firmly upon the formal features of the model, consequently there is little place for a detailed exemplification of particular features by reference to examples of current practice. What I am offering is a model that others can help me to test against the reality of what is done in actual class-rooms.[25] Until we have such a model, a whole heap of examples will tell us very little, whatever their individual excellence as practice, because we will have no means of knowing in general terms what is really going on in 'English' classes and no means of comparing one example of practice with another.

The model makes use of four basic categories, OBJECTIVES, AIMS, PROCESSES and APPROACHES. Something has already been said about the relationship of OBJECTIVES to AIMS and I suggested that it is analogous to the relationship of elements to structure as these terms are used in describing the patterns of natural languages. I mentioned, however, that we had to consider the existence of a further level of organisation active in shaping our choice of elements and structure. Just as we can reasonably ask *why* we make one selection from the grammar of a natural language rather than another, so we can ask why a teacher should make one selection from the grammar of English practice rather than another. What is needed is a term for the level of conceptual organisation which determines the teacher's actual selection of OBJECTIVES and AIMS. This term is provided by the concept of an APPROACH.

Another way of looking at the relationship between OBJECTIVES and AIMS on the one hand, and APPROACHES on the other, is to make use of the distinction between foreground and background, a MICRO and a MACRO level of effective organisation of class-room operations.[26] MICRO and MACRO are borrowed from the realm of life science, in particular from ecology, where the biologist talks about MICRO and MACRO environments. A typical MICRO environment would be a garden wall or pond, while a MACRO environment would be provided by deserts, or coniferous forests, or the sea. Applied to teaching, obviously the MICRO environment is best seen as the individual class-room, whereas the key MACRO environments are furnished by the curriculum, the educational system and the value system of society at large. In terms of the model I am putting forward, APPROACHES are a MACRO feature, while OBJECTIVES and AIMS are features which mediate between general ideas about the nature and function of English and the MICRO level of the individual class-room situation, where they are realised by particular activities and procedures.

There is one aspect of this decision-making process, however, that has not yet been examined. A key element in the teacher's MACRO view of English is the view he takes of the activity of learning itself. He has to ask himself what kind of an answer he would give to the question, '*How* do pupils learn?' as well as the more obvious and expected question, '*What* should they learn?' and '*Why* should they learn it?' This aspect of his thinking is *part* of his APPROACH, but it is not synonymous with it. We must therefore distinguish it within our model and this gives us our fourth category of PROCESS. PROCESS points to the fact that learning is a dynamic activity, a question of *becoming*, and that everything we do in the class-room is a reflection of our view of that activity.

What I have said so far about the formal properties of the model is only a bare sketch. I do not want to develop it any further at this stage, however, as it would involve a very different kind of discussion from the one that I hope to promote. What follows is, therefore, no more than a working summary of these properties, sufficient to support the more detailed discussion of the four categories of the model which follow. As these discussions lead to a considerable amount of systematic differentiation within each category, I have included a table of Section III as a guide.

1   The basic categories of the model
OBJECTIVES
AIMS
PROCESSES
APPROACHES

70

2 *Objectives and aims*
   OBJECTIVES for English.
   AIMS   Class I   —focused upon the needs of the learner.
                Class II —focused upon the needs of society.
                Class III—focused upon the transmission of values.

3 *Processes*
   I   —DEVELOPMENTAL
   II —INSTRUMENTAL
   III—HEURISTIC

4 *Approaches*
   I   —PERSONAL: i—Individualistic
                        ii—Experientialistic
   II —INSTRUMENTAL: i—Pragmatic
                        ii—Moralistic
                        iii—Academic
   III—RIGORISTIC and HUMANISTIC modes of all three
       INSTRUMENTAL approaches.

OBJECTIVE. An OBJECTIVE is a MEDIATORY feature. It relates to the
day-to-day states of affairs that are to be found within a particular context; in this case, the pattern of learning in an English
class. They are *subject* specific and answer the question 'What
is this detail of the pattern primarily for, given that its aim is x?'
In this sense, it is the OBJECTIVE which immediately determines
the content of a lesson. It is a formal feature which provides the
answer to some particular question about what is to be done.
It does not itself assert *why* that particular thing should be done,
however, or *how* it should be done, though any objective may
in practice have a direct bearing on how a teacher chooses to
answer these questions. OBJECTIVES, therefore, cannot, of themselves, assist in determining why a teacher does x rather than y:
they can only state that x does occur as one of the OBJECTIVES
which can be shown to shape his practice.

AIM. An AIM is also a MEDIATORY feature. It is relational, but
system, rather than subject, specific, for it is an attempt to answer
such questions as 'What am I teaching English for?' or 'What
is a curriculum for?' AIMS may have implications for content,
but they do not determine it. They relate a content to some more

71

abstract value such as 'the pursuit of knowledge' or 'the development of the whole man'.

APPROACH. An APPROACH is a MACRO feature. That is to say, the name for a principle or concept or high-level value which leads a teacher to determine upon one particular concatenation of AIMS and OBJECTIVES rather than another as the guiding principle of his practice. It is more than just the sum of the OBJECTIVES and AIMS associated with its selection, however. An APPROACH is a *principled basis for the selection* of OBJECTIVES and AIMS and is therefore an evaluative concept, answering the question WHY in relation to both: why these OBJECTIVES rather than those; why these AIMS rather than those; and consequently, why is the educational system to be used in this way rather than that, in so far as this area of the curriculum is concerned?

PROCESS. A PROCESS is a MICRO feature. It describes what is done in a given context in relation to the pursuit of a given objective. It is system specific, but not general: that is to say, it does not have meaning except in a particular learning environment, and that learning environment is provided by (a) a specific area of the curriculum and (b) specific AIMS and OBJECTIVES, so that, in talking about PROCESS, it is always necessary to make statements of the form, 'In the context x, given OBJECTIVES $y1 \ldots yn$, and AIMS $\zeta1 \ldots \zeta n$, the process P is made use of.' A PROCESS cannot, therefore, define its own value as a contribution to a learning situation or its aptness to the pursuit of any particular objective. The concept of PROCESS embraces both activities and procedures.[27]

2   Objectives and aims in English practice

In giving a summary outline of these two categories at the end of the last section, I suggested that OBJECTIVES were subject specific, while AIMS were system specific. The distinction implied here is fundamental to the design of this model. Objectives are subject specific, because they arise from the fact that a teacher is involved with a particular 'content', whether or not that 'content' is dignified in the curriculum by the name of Subject. When a teacher of English finds himself operating in a context of Combined Studies or even Integrated Studies, his objectives, in so far as he is a teacher of

English, derive from the fact that his contribution in these areas is marked by one particular view of reality rather than another. In plain language, to teach at all you have to teach *something*, and it is that something which determines your objectives.

AIMS on the other hand I have described as being system specific. I have referred frequently in this paper to the educational system and to the curriculum itself as a system. In both cases, what is implied is that we can best talk about a particular area of human activity if we regard it as being in some sense autonomous. In other words, once in being it creates particular rules and conventions which govern performance of certain activities and particular contexts in which those activities can be carried on. In our case, teaching is governed by the rules and conventions of the educational system at one level, and the particular social and pedagogic organisation of individual schools and colleges at another. At the same time, what is taught is governed by the set of rules and conventions which we call the curriculum. Whereas the educational system creates contexts in which teaching is carried on, contexts which I have called in this book 'learning situations', the curriculum creates the contexts in which knowledge is made available for learning. It can therefore be seen that the 'educational system' and 'the curriculum' are both systems.[28]

In Section Two I suggested that the teacher's aim '... is what guides the actual pattern of work he devises to meet the needs of the situation' (p. 66). It is for this reason that I have described AIMS as *mediatory* features. In the teacher's mind they go between what at this stage we will simply call 'the demands of the system' on the one hand, and 'the exigencies of the learning situation' on the other. OBJECTIVES are also *mediatory* features, but their function is to go between 'the demands of the subject' and 'the exigencies of the learning situation'.

I give now a representative selection of the kinds of OBJECTIVES which currently determine the day-to-day practice of teachers of English. This selection is merely intended to illustrate what I understand by objectives and does not claim to be in any sense exhaustive.

(1) Encouraging the growth of moral sensibility.

(2) Mediating aspects of high culture and the values embodied therein through the study of 'the best that has been thought and said'.
(3) Developing the individual self by talking and writing about personal experience.
(4) Encouraging the growth of social awareness (sociological perspective):[29] the capacity to evaluate patterns of social action and judge for oneself the validity of current norms and conventions governing social behaviour.
(5) Inculcating specific linguistic skills, 'the tools for the job', seen as ends in themselves, or as a necessary means for the successful pursuit of learning activities in other areas of the curriculum.
(6) Developing 'communicative competence'; the ability to understand the words of others, spoken or written, and to make ourselves understood in return.
(7) Inculcating the norms of 'polite' usage as the objective correlative for 'maintaining standards,' whether linguistic or social.
(8) Developing the social self: encouraging growth of the individual's fluency as a participant in social action, that is, his capacity to handle a wide range of social situations, especially unfamiliar ones.[30]

The problem in describing AIMS is the level of generality involved once the attempt is made to formulate them explicitly. If the level adopted is too high, then the formulation is emptied of useful meaning, because the aim so described would be capable of covering too wide a field and thus embrace so large a number of disparate elements that drawing them together within one category would cease to have point. This would be the case were we to say that, for instance, the aim of education was to mediate values. To say this would offer no clue as to *what* values, from *what* sources, and whether or not they were all to be considered as *essentially* the same kind of thing, mediated in the same way. On the other hand, were one merely to make a list of the values that are somehow associated with the concept of education in our society, the result would be equally uninteresting, because each value we mentioned would then appear to stand on its own. It would have to be considered as an instance independently of all the others, so that our hope for particularity would end up by leaving us without a significant level of generality for our statements. While this might satisfy some teachers, as it would appear to demonstrate the futility of trying to say anything about the practice of education that went beyond the narrative record of work done, it is scarcely a tenable position. It ignores the point we have already made that common sense suggests all teachers of English might be expected to share something in common by virtue of the fact that they were indeed all teachers of English.

The present model offers a solution to this problem by treating AIMS as *discrete formal features* rather than as all-embracing concepts. The attitudes, assumptions and ideas that combine to make up a teacher's view of his role as a teacher will therefore include a number of aims. AIMS are, however, only one set of features out of several which go to make up the teacher's APPROACH. This means that we must not expect to find *an* aim turning up on its own in the real context of a class-room, or curriculum, context. What we must look for is the way in which aims cluster and the weight which is given to any one aim in the clustering, relative to any other. It is this cluster of AIMS which provides the means by which the broad and general ideas informing a teacher's APPROACH at the MACRO level can be related to the objectives that he sets before himself, and thus the particular selection of activities and procedures he chooses for a particular learning situation at the MICRO level. Thus it is that a teacher's aims can be said to provide the principled basis for his decision-making at the MICRO level of moment-to-moment interaction between teacher and class throughout the progress of a lesson, and in the day-to-day planning of particular activities and procedures for particular lessons.

What follows, therefore, is an outline of the individual AIMS which are currently most predominant in the practice of English Teaching rather than an attempt to account for the way in which they cluster in the real situation created by the educational system and the curriculum. Were we to look at the way in which aims cluster, we would be testing hypotheses generated by the model rather than describing the model itself and that would be beyond the scope of this book.

There is one further point to make about AIMS in contrast to OBJECTIVES. We have said already that aims are system specific. What this means in practice is that when we come to write them down on paper we have to formulate them in such a way that they will be applicable across the curriculum. Consequently, if we are focused on a particular area of the curriculum such as English, we have to think about the shape that any one particular AIM is likely to take on in the curriculum context of English rather than any other curriculum context. We cannot, as we can with OBJECTIVES, show the 'Englishness' of the aim in the formulation of the aim itself.

Three classes of AIM are set up on the basis of a fundamental difference in perspective as to what the educational system is to be used for. The aims which are included within each class do not, of course, exhaust its potential membership. The aims set down for each class should be regarded as representative of all those that could properly be considered members of it. In passing, it can be said that the most obvious reason for this potential open-endedness is that aims change continuously in relation to the changing patterns and pressures of the society within which the educational system in question has its being.[31]

Class I   Those aims which focus upon the need for the educational system to put at its centre the child as learner and are therefore most concerned with the development of the individual self.[32]
   (1) To work from each pupil's existing experience of the world.
   (2) To take account of the particular needs of each individual pupil, both personal and educational.
   (3) To develop whatever potential for learning a pupil may possess, both formal and informal.
   (4) To provide for the development of whatever imaginative and aesthetic capacity a pupil may posess.
   (5) To encourage the capacity to exercise personal judgement, based upon a pupil's ability to read the meaning of his own experience of the world.

Class II   Those aims which focus upon the need for the educational system to sustain the fabric of society.[33]
   (1) To inculcate basic skills, primarily the capacity to use written language and to read written texts.
   (2) To impart the useful knowledge deemed to be necessary for the effective day-to-day running of a complex industrial society.
   (3) To transmit those advanced knowledges which provide the basis for the technology of a complex industrial society.

(4) To regulate access to 'the commanding heights' of such a society, the professions, management and the government.

(5) To teach those who are deemed capable of thinking, how to think: and those who cannot, how to accept the decisions of those who can. That is, to inculcate in the majority a willing acceptance of the regulatory function of the minority.

Class III   Those aims which focus upon the need for the educational system to function as a mediator of values, intellectual, moral, social and cultural.

(1) To maintain the integrity of the discipline: the concept of knowledge as necessarily organised territorially in terms of fields, bodies, areas and subjects.[34]

(2) To maintain the integrity of an aspect of high culture, in this case literature, and mediate values which are believed to be solely contained therein.[35]

(3) To transmit the accumulated 'wisdom of the tribe' concerning the nature of intellectual, moral, social and cultural reality.

(4) To maintain the integrity of the existing social order by acting as an agency through which individuals are socialised into accepting the value systems embodied in the *status quo*.[36]

(5) To induce in the majority a proper deference to the values of the minority and a parallel acceptance of this minority dominating 'the commanding heights'.

3   Processes in relation to English practice

PROCESSES cannot be described in the same way as AIMS or OBJECTIVES. It is not feasible to give a list of processes, because the range of activities and procedures which teachers select in order to realise a particular process in their class-rooms is so varied. What can be done, however, is to outline what we may call the pedagogic bias, or direction, of the process type which a teacher makes use of. This will remind us that a process is not so much a mental event in the mind of the teacher, as is the case with aims and objectives, as a pragmatical answer, in terms of activities and procedures, to two questions: 'What must I do as a teacher, if my pupils are to learn?'; and 'What must pupils do as individual learners, if they are to realise the potential within them for the acquisition of knowledge?'

Broadly, these questions encourage the setting up of three major classes of PROCESS, the DEVELOPMENTAL, the INSTRUCTIONAL and the HEURISTIC.

The DEVELOPMENTAL. Here learning is a function of personal growth, hence the guiding principle for the teacher is the local and individual needs and responses of individual pupils. He seeks to create situations in which new experience can be met and responded to in such a way that what is learnt is how to respond to that experience. Processes from this class imply that learning has taken place when pupils can answer for themselves, *in their own terms*, the question: 'What is it to know what we experience?'

The INSTRUCTIONAL. Here learning is a function of the acquisition of a recognised body of knowledge, hence the guiding principle for the teacher is the need to present that body of knowledge in such a way that it is accessible to his pupils, while ensuring that it remains recognisable as a body of knowledge. He creates situations in which knowledge is *transduced*, rather than translated or reinterpreted. The focus of instructional processes tends to be, therefore, a focus upon *what* is acquired, not *how* it is learnt: it is a question of the pupil's knowing that x is so and not otherwise, rather than his being able to focus upon the process of learning that that state of affairs is the case. Processes of this type suggest, therefore, that learning has taken place when pupils can answer for themselves, *in the terms appropriate to the discipline*, the question: 'What has to be known in order to be accounted knowledgeable?'

The HEURISTIC. Here learning is a function of the acquisition of knowledge, personally motivated. The guiding principle for the teacher is the pupil's need to see for himself the meaningfulness of what he learns in relation to a context that is exterior to the organisation of his own self. The teacher creates situations which aim to show that 'x is so and not otherwise', as with INSTRUCTIONAL processes, but does so in such a way that this is the product of the pupil's involvement in the process of moving from what is known to what is not known. Processes of this type therefore suggest that learning has taken place when pupils can answer for themselves, *in terms that reconcile their own understanding of the case with that represented by the discipline*, the question: 'How can we come to know what we want to know?'[37]

78

Processes determine *how* things are done, not *what* is done or *why* it is done, so that they do have a direct influence on relationships in the learning situation.

DEVELOPMENTAL processes express the underlying operational assumption that the activity of learning can only take place in so far as the teacher leaves the pupil free from limitation or constraint, so that he can make use of the capabilities innate within him. Learning is not so much a process of acquisition as of recognition.

With INSTRUCTIONAL processes, on the other hand, the underlying operational assumption is that the activity of learning can only take place in so far as the teacher initiates a process involving the acquisition of knowledge that, by definition, the pupils are deemed ignorant of. Learning is virtually synonymous, at the school level, with 'knowing the facts', and 'the facts' that are to be known are predetermined by the needs of discipline rather than the needs of the learner.

HEURISTIC processes express an underlying assumption that, while the activity of learning can only take place if there is significant acquisition of new information, the activity itself implies a predisposition in the learner to discover what is new, and that the teacher's task is to create situations in which pupils come to learn how to make use of this predisposition. In other words, his processes will express the fact that learning is primarily a matter of *learning how to learn*; that the capacity to do so is innate in the human animal; and that knowledge is the product of relating what is new to what is known in such a way that the new enters into a syntactic relationship with the known.

4 Approaches in relation to English

As I suggested at the beginning of this section when we come to consider the teacher's APPROACH we are concerned with concepts at a very high level of abstraction. This means that the way they are describable is likely to show even fewer signs of the specific area of the curriculum concerned than was the case with AIMS or APPROACHES. The reason for this is not hard to see if we go back to our idea that AIMS and APPROACHES were mediating between the

79

MICRO level of the actual learning situation and the MACRO level of a teacher's fundamental orientation towards the practice of his role as a teacher.

It will be remembered that it was necessary to set up a category of APPROACH in order to account for the fact that a teacher's choice of AIMS and OBJECTIVES had to be made somewhere. The level at which it was made had to be able to admit questions of value. In effect, it was suggested that the teacher derives from his APPROACH, his broad orientation towards the 'activity of educating', his concrete decisions about activities and procedures by making use of the middle-order mediatory concepts we have called AIMS and OBJECTIVES.

In the same way, we can now suggest that approaches have to come from somewhere. While the majority of teachers would regard their own approach as somehow 'obvious' or 'natural', this cannot be accepted as a satisfactory account of the matter, once it is agreed that there are several approaches to be found governing the practice of teachers even in one area of the curriculum. This is an enormous topic and I only touch on it here in order to underline the necessary abstractness of the idea of an approach. Were I to develop it in detail, I would want to show that just as AIMS and OBJECTIVES mediate between a teacher's APPROACH and his classroom practice, so in effect, at another level, APPROACHES mediate between ideas, attitudes and assumptions active in the culture and a teacher's concept of his professional role as a teacher.

It is possible to distinguish between major types of approach, in terms of a difference of perspective between those that are primarily concerned with the interior economy of the child's states of feeling and knowing, and those that focus upon his relationship to states of affairs external to himself. What discriminates between approaches, therefore, is the kind of answer an approach would provide to the basic question: 'What is required for a pupil to be an .../do an .../know an .../feel an ...?' The way in which a teacher answers these questions will lead him to very different sets of criteria for decision-making in learning situations as to relevant activities and procedures and to very different ways of evaluating the activity which follows from their adoption.

I PERSONAL APPROACHES

The Individualistic

In this version of the PERSONAL approach, the teacher's bias is towards the immediate and individual needs and responses of individual pupils. What is done in the class-room is always finally related to the question, 'What is needed for *this* pupil to realise his potential as a "whole man", as an integrated and developed personality?' The answer is always given in terms of individual growth rather than social obligation.

The Experientialistic

In this version of the PERSONAL approach, the teacher's bias is towards the existing experience that pupils bring into the class-room with them. The point of departure is always pupils' pre-existing knowledge of the world. Any one step forward in terms of the new must not be so great as to open up a credibility gap between what is known and what can be conceived of as knowable.

Features common to both forms of the PERSONAL approach are a pervasive emphasis upon what is thought of as 'imaginative', upon the 'very culture of the feelings',[38] and upon the need to accept that education must necessarily be child-centred in order to be in any sense education. These two approaches are much more closely related to each other than the three which follow. In a sense, they represent alternative ways of focusing upon a common theme, education as a process for developing the individual's consciousness of an individuated self.

II INSTRUMENTAL APPROACHES

The Pragmatic

In this approach the teacher's attention is directed away from the interior state of the individual's consciousness and towards his needs in relation to society. The basic question the teacher asks himself is, 'What is it necessary for pupils to know if they are to operate successfully as members of society?' He will ask this question in relation to the local environment of the school, and in relation to the larger environment of the world beyond school, both in the sense of the pupil's life as a member of his community while at school and his future life as an adult after school.

As the teacher's point of departure is his desire to provide his pupils with a particular *operational* capacity, work in the class-room will be powerfully shaped by his view of what capacities are necessary to meet the demands of the educational system and the society within which he is operating as a teacher. Consequently, his practice will tend to be dominated by the various criteria set up to govern access to different levels of the educational system and to the various agencies within society. He accepts as a major constraint on his practice as a teacher that the school has an overriding obligation to provide pupils with the means of satisfying those criteria.

The Moralistic
In this approach the teacher sees himself primarily as the one whose task it is to transmit and to maintain the cultural values which he believes to be necessary for the survival of his society. The teacher, as the active agent in the educational process, is seen to occupy a crucial position. He views himself, not so much as the means by which pupils gain access to the knowledge systems of their society, but as the key figure through whom they have access to the approved value systems of their society.

As the teacher's point of departure is his desire to induct his pupils into a particular moral universe, work in the class-room will be powerfully shaped by his view of what constitutes for him right action and right thinking. His practice will be dominated by his desire to put before his pupils evidence of only those views of reality of which he approves, or create conditions in which his pupils are constrained to accept his valuation of the views of reality of which he does not approve.[39]

It needs to be said that the above formulation applies as much to the natural and social sciences as it does to the humanities. A reader may like to consider for himself how a teacher with a moralistic approach would handle such topics as economic aid for under-developed countries, the controversy over heredity and environment or, in the matter sciences, the nature of scientific enquiry.[40]

The Academic
In this approach the teacher sees himself primarily as one whose task it is to pass on to teach each new generation of pupils the intellectual knowledge in his keeping. His chief concern, therefore, is

with what we may call 'the integrity of knowing'. This is to say that he is very closely focused upon the difference between the world of commonsensical, or experiential, knowing and the kind of knowing which has to do with hypotheses about states of affairs, whether linguistic, literary, historical, geographical, social, biological or physical, and the kinds of criteria by which they are to be assessed as true or false. What is done in the class-room, therefore, is determined by a teacher's understanding of the nature of a subject discipline and how he sees his pupils in relation to their ignorance of the field concerned. What is to be learnt is determined by reference to the interior economy of the discipline rather than the interior economy of the learner.

Whereas a *pragmatical* approach is dominated by considerations of useful/non-useful: a *moralistic* approach is dominated by considerations of right/wrong: and an *academic* approach by considerations of true/false.

If we were now to look more closely at the PRAGMATIC approach, we would discover that it was necessary to account for a marked difference of perspective occurring amongst those who are guided in their practice by this approach. There are important differences between the practice of those who accept, let us say, the existing criteria for entry to different levels of the educational system as a valid and proper measure of what pupils should be taught, and those who first ask what it is that pupils need in order to be successful within the existing system, and then set out to provide it. The former are likely to bend the pupil to meet the demands of the system, while the latter are more likely to see their task as mediating between the demands of the system and the needs of particular groups of learners.[41]

We can recognise this difference of perspective by talking about a RIGORISTIC and a HUMANISTIC mode of the PRAGMATIC approach. For example, in relation to the use of written English, a RIGORISTIC PRAGMATIC approach would insist on the need to 'maintain standards', with the implication that standards of written English were uniform for the use of the written language throughout our society: and that these standards were given once and for all, and were clearly discernible for all educated users of the language. A teacher adopting this mode of the PRAGMATIC approach would tend to

83

present what he took to be the values enshrined in the idea of 'good English',[42] and induce pupils to adopt, accept and exercise patterns of usage which realised the norms embodied in that idea of good English. The underlying assumption is that the pupil must be given a code for correct usage if he is to play his part successfully in society.

A teacher adopting the HUMANISTIC mode of this approach, however, would be likely to emphasise the *conventionality* of all standards, with the implication that standards of usage arise out of particular kinds of linguistic activity in particular contexts. He would suggest that the relevance of particular 'standards' to particular contexts was a matter for critical evaluation rather than uncritical acceptance. He would present the concept of 'good English' as a function of what Goffman[43] calls a 'working consensus', that which is necessary if the individuals coming together on a particular occasion to do a particular job are to be able to carry it out.

The underlying assumption of a HUMANISTIC PRAGMATIC approach is that pupils must be given access to strategies which would enable them to work out for themselves what usage is relevant for any of the multiplicity of contexts in which they are likely to find themselves, while the RIGORISTIC PRAGMATIC approach would insist that 'good usage' is uniform and can be taught as a set of rules, universal in their application. Whichever of these two modes is involved, however, the teacher's basis for decision and evaluation in the class-room situation arises out of his need to relate whatever is done there to some measure of what is currently being demanded of individuals in their capacity as players of social roles, whether as pupils, as members of a community, or as future adult members of a complex industrial society.

If we now consider our other two types of approach, the MORALISTIC and the ACADEMIC, we shall discover that it is possible to distinguish a similar difference of perspective in each case. This suggests that the distinction between what I have described as a RIGORISTIC and a HUMANISTIC perspective has general validity in terms of how teachers view their function as teachers. Again, the pursuit of this topic would carry us away from our main purpose, which is to present, rather than to exemplify, a formal model for the

84

description and evaluation of 'English' in the curriculum. It should be said, however, that these terms can be related to Durkheim's notions of 'mechanical' and 'organic' solidarity respectively.[44] A RIGORISTIC perspective implies a belief in an implicit value system and its indefinite perpetuation in the life of the community, hence it seeks to minimise individual differences: while a HUMANISTIC perspective assumes the need for explicit systems of values, because it accepts the fact of individual difference, consequently it opens up the possibility of reviewing those values, and therefore the probability that they will change. Seen from a RIGORISTIC perspective, society is unchanging and it is the duty of the teacher to fit the pupil to its patterns. Seen from a HUMANISTIC perspective, society is both plural and changeable, and therefore it is the duty of the teacher to equip the pupil to meet the continuously changing demands it will make upon him.

If we now look again at the MORALISTIC and ACADEMIC approaches, we can suggest in outline what this difference of perspective might look like with regard to each of them. The RIGORISTIC MORALISTIC is very familiar. In some ways, it has been the approach most favoured within our own educational system, and indeed, within the educational systems of other Western European countries also. A teacher adopting this approach believes he holds in trust values without the passing on of which civilisation, as understood by the dominant group within his society, will founder. What is done or used in the class-room will always be related to the developing of sound principles for right action as interpreted in the light of these values. It will be obvious from this description that the Arnoldian tradition was very much an expression of this approach. In practice, the emphasis has always been upon the acquisition, rather than the examination, of the received values of the community. Pupils' performance in school, moreover, is likely to be assessed by how well they behave rather than how effectively they think.

A HUMANISTIC MORALISTIC approach, on the other hand, would lead a teacher to lay emphasis on the fact that behaviour was determined by how individuals choose to act, and that standards of behaviour derive from the quality of individual moral choices. He would be pointing to the fact that the basis for moral choice was not so much the ability to apply a set of rules which have been derived from the received values of a society, or social group, as the ability to

85

examine critically the issues involved in that choice and the implications for both the individual, and for the community, of the alternatives it presents.

Finally, we can consider this difference of perspective in relation to the ACADEMIC instrumental approach. A teacher adopting a RIGORISTIC perspective would tend to regard what is known as given, and his primary function in the learning situation as the presentation of what is known. The pupil would be considered ignorant until in possession of the facts, but this 'knowing of the facts' would not put him in a position which justified his being allowed to comment on the facts, because 'the facts' available to the pupil will always be so small a fraction of the 'body of knowledge' which constitutes the discipline in question. In these terms, the RIGORISTIC ACADEMIC approach leads a teacher to view the educational process as an indefinite regression, for he will only account as 'knowledgeable' those in full possession of 'the facts'; and comment is only possible for someone who is knowledgeable. Those whom he believes to know enough to be called 'knowledgeable', however, always exist one stage further on in the educational process. In effect, the teacher denies to his pupil the right to comment, because the pupil is not 'knowledgeable' in relation to the teacher's command of 'the facts'; but the teacher also denies himself the right to comment, because he does not account himself 'knowledgeable' in relation to the discipline.[45]

On the other hand a HUMANISTIC ACADEMIC approach regards 'the facts' as the product of a process of enquiry into states of affairs so as to discover what might be the case. A teacher adopting this approach would tend to see his function as the construction of situations by means of which the pupil can explore states of affairs in order to find out for himself what is true about them. This does involve presentation of 'the facts', but the presentation is governed by the desire to show that 'the facts' are not given but made. The pupil is ignorant, until he has been given the chance to find out what is the case. The movement from being ignorant to being knowledgeable, however, is a function of the interaction between the pupil's prior knowledge of the world and the unfamiliar states of affairs he is asked to explore. Comment is therefore a necessary element in the process of learning, because, however small the body

86

of fact known to the pupil, comparison with what he already knows about the world provides a valid basis for comment.

In these terms the HUMANISTIC, like the RIGORISTIC, academic approach sees the educational process as an indefinite regression. In this case, however, it is because no one can ever be in full possession of the facts.[46] Knowledge is a process of making sense out of what one has, hence comment is the objective correlative for 'being knowledgeable' in the process of learning, because it mediates between what is known and what is new. Within this HUMANISTIC mode of the ACADEMIC approach, a teacher is likely to operate in the learning situation on the assumption that there is always a possibility of relevant comment available to his pupils, provided that the teacher takes into account the existing range of their knowledge of the relevant states of affairs.

In this outline of the categories of the model, I have tried to show how the various elements in the teacher's view of his responsibilities relate to each other. In the form that I have given to the exemplification of aims, objectives, procedures and approaches I have tried to suggest a way of talking about them that is public in its language and professional in its orientation. At the same time, the model puts forward a number of hypotheses about teacher attitudes and assumptions in a way which is eminently testable, given the necessary resources. What I hope I have been able to do, therefore, is to show how a model of this kind can be immediately useful to teachers, because it provides them with new ways of thinking through the basis of their day-to-day decision-making in the class-room. At the same time, the model could be the point of departure for an extended enquiry into the theory and practice of English. Given the generality of its categories, however, my ultimate hope is that many people might find it useful in carrying forward the searching review of theory and practice across the curriculum which is the essential task of the decade for all those actively involved in the process of education in this country and elsewhere.

REFERENCES

1. For a discussion of competence, see Part I, p. 45.
2. For a discussion of these ideas, see Doughty (1968) (b).
3. The classic statement of this position remains F. R. Leavis' *Education and the University*. Of all the more recent restatements, the one that expresses the essence of this position in terms closest to the class-room is David Holbrook's *English for Maturity*.
4. See the chapter on literature in Whitehead (1966), *English in Education*, ed. by Brian Jackson and Denys Thomson, and the files of the journal *The Use of English*, Chatto and Windus.
5. The best-considered exposition of this view is Creber (1965).
6. The relationship between an educational system and its society is explored in Doughty and Thornton (1972), Ch. 1, sect. iii.
7. The following two paragraphs contain an outline of the argument presented in Doughty and Thornton (1972), Ch. 1, sect. iii. See also Bernstein (1971) for the underlying theory of social learning implied.
8. Doughty, Pearce and Thornton (1972), p. 8.
9. Del Hymes (1968).
10. Doughty and Thornton (1972), Ch. 2, sect. ii.
11. Much information on this matter emerged in the course of the fieldwork done during the development stage of the *Language in Use* project.
12. See Part I, p. 9.
13. For this use of 'cultural learning' in the context of attitudes to language, see Doughty, Peter and Anne (1974), Ch. 3.
14. Doughty, Peter and Anne (1974). See also Doughty, Pearce and Thornton (1972), pp. 27 et seq.
15. A readily accessible account will be found in Sprott (1967), or his paper, 'Society: what is it and how does it change?' in *Basic Readings in the Sociology of Education*, ed. Swift, Student Library of Education (1970), R.K.P.
16. See Doughty, Pearce and Thornton (1972), p. 100.
17. Young (1970). For the theory of social learning which underlies this passage, see Bernstein (1971), *Social class, language and civilisation*.
18. Halliday (1973). See also, Chomsky (1964), pp. 9 et seq.
19. See Part I, pp. 12 et seq.
20. In addition to the above references, see also Lyons (1968), Halliday (1970) and Crystal (1971), pp. 77 et seq.
21. For the idea of 'realise', see Halliday (1973), p. 30.
22. Halliday (1973), 'Semantics and syntax in a functional theory of language.'
23. cf. the discussion of the 'Progressive consensus' approach in section 2 of Part I.
24. Gurney (1973).

25. I have referred to this idea of 'testing' in Part I, p. 8. The most accessible account of what I have in mind is Medawar (1967), 'Hypothesis and Imagination', the most profound Popper (1963).
26. I was helped to this formulation by a paper of David Jenkins of the Keele Humanities Project, given to open Commission 6 of the York International Conference, 1971.
27. See Doughty, Pearce and Thornton (1971), p. 9.
28. I have been much influenced in my thinking in this area by the essays in Young (1971), esp. Bernstein, 'On the classification and framing of educational knowledge'.
29. See Berger (1963).
30. See especially, *Half our Future*, H.M.S.O. (1963), pp. 152 et seq.
31. For this concept of change see Doughty and Thornton (1972), pp. 33 et seq. and Postman and Weingartner (1969).
32. This class of aims seems to have been predominant in the thinking of the Plowden commission on Primary Education, *Children and Their Primary Schools*, H.M.S.O. (1967). See Peters (1969). Also Dearden (1968), esp. Chs. 2, 3, and 4.
33. This class of aims seems to have been uppermost in the minds of those who contributed seriously to the *Critical Quarterly*'s Black Papers.
34. cf. Jacques Barzun, *The House of Intellect* (1959).
35. Leavis (1943).
36. For a critique of this position, see Postman and Weingartner (1971).
37. The best brief account of this process is still Bruner (1965), but see also Jones (1972) for a necessary 'Yes, but . . .'
38. cf. Holbrook (1961), pp. 39 et seq.
39. For the idea of alternative 'realities' see Berger and Luckman (1966). See also Bernstein (1971), Introduction.
40. An interesting example is discussed by Liam Hudson, 'The context of the debate' in *Race, Culture and Intelligence*, ed. Richardson and Speers, Penguin (1972). For a critique of the *moralistic* nature of 'objective' enquiry, see Polanyi (1958).
41. cf. Postman and Weingartner (1969), pp. 15 et seq.
42. Doughty (1968) (b).
43. Goffman (1959), p. 80.
44. For 'mechanical' and 'organic' solidarity see Aron (1967), p. 21. Also Durkheim himself (1933), Chs. 2 and 3.
45. See Bernstein in Young (1971).
46. Popper (1963).

Bibliography

Aron, Raymond (1967), *Main Currents in Sociological Thought. 2.* Penguin.

Bannister, D. and Fay Fransella (1971), *Inquiring Man: The theory of personal constructs*, Penguin.

Bantock, G. H. (1971), 'Towards a theory of popular education' in *Times Educational Supplement*. 12.3.1971.

Barzun, Jacques (1959), *The House of Intellect*, Secker and Warburg.

Berger, Peter I, (1963), *Invitation to Sociology*, Penguin.

Berger, Peter and Thomas Luckman (1966), *The Social Construction of Reality*, Penguin University Books.

Bernstein, Basil (1971), *Class, Codes and Control, Vol. 1.*, Routledge and Kegan Paul.

Bernstein, Basil (1972), *Class, Codes and Control, Vol. 2.*, Routledge and Kegan Paul.

Britton, James (1970), *Language and Learning*, Penguin Press.

Booth, Wayne (1971), 'Centre of all intellectual development', *Times Educational Supplement*, 26.11.1971.

Bruner, Jerome S. (1965), *The Process of Education*, Harvard University Press.

Chomsky, Noam (1964), *Current Issues in Linguistic Theory*, Mouton and Co.

Cox, C. B. and Dyson, A. E., Editors, *Black Paper One*. 'Fight for Education'. March 1969. *Black Paper Two*, 'The Crisis in Education'. The Critical Quarterly Society.

Creber, J. W. Patrick (1965), *Sense and Sensitivity*, University of London Press.

Creber, J. W. Patrick (1972), *Lost for Words*, Penguin.

Crystal, David (1971), *Linguistics*, Penguin.

Dearden, R. F. (1968), *The Philosophy of Primary Education*, Routledge and Kegan Paul.

Dixon, John (1967), *Growth through English*, Oxford University Press, London.

Doughty, Peter Paper 1, *The relevance of linguistics for the teacher of English*, Programme in Linguistics and English Teaching, Longmans.

Doughty, Peter (1968), Paper 4, *Current attitudes to written English, and the implication for the teacher of English*, Programme in Linguistics and English Teaching, Longmans.

Doughty, Peter (1968), Paper 5, *Linguistics and the teaching of literature*, Programme in Linguistics and English Teaching, Longmans.

Doughty, Peter, Geoffrey Thornton and John Pearce (1971), *Language in Use*, Edward Arnold.

Doughty, Peter, Geoffrey Thornton and John Pearce, (1972) *Exploring Language*, Edward Arnold.

Doughty, Peter and Geoffrey Thornton (1973), *Language Study, the Teacher and the learner,* Edward Arnold.

Doughty, Peter (1972), 'Pupils also use language to live: a defence of a linguistic approach to language study for the classroom', *English in Education,* Vol. 6. No. 1., Spring 1972, Chatto and Windus.

Doughty, Peter and Anne Doughty (1974), *Language and Community,* Edward Arnold.

Durkheim, Emile (1947), *The Division of Labor in Society,* Collier-Macmillan.

Firth, J. R. (1957), *Papers in Linguistics 1934–1951,* Oxford University Press.

Ford, Boris (1965), *Who teaches English?,* N.A.T.E. Bulletin, Vol. 2. No. 2., Summer 1965.

Fries, Charles C. (1957), *The Structure of English,* Longmans.

Goffman, Erving (1969), *The Presentation of Self in Everyday Life,* Allen Lane, The Penguin Press.

Gurney, Roger (1973), *Language, Brain and Interactive Processes,* Edward Arnold.

Halliday, M. A. K. (1970), 'Language Structure and Language Function' in *New Horizons in Linguistics,* Penguin.

Halliday, M. A. K. H. (1973), *Explorations in the Functions of Language,* Edward Arnold.

Hanson, Norwood Russell (1958), *Patterns of Discovery,* Cambridge University Press.

Hannam, Charles, Pat Smyth and Norman Stephenson (1971), *Young Teachers and Reluctant Learners,* Penguin 1971.

H.M.S.O. (1963), *Half Our Future, A report of the Central Advisory Council for Education.*

Holbrook, David (1961), *English for Maturity,* Cambridge University Press.

Holbrook, David (1964), *English for the Rejected,* Cambridge University Press.

Hymes, Del (1968), 'The Ethnography of Speaking', in *Readings in the Sociology of Language,* ed. Joshua A. Fishman, Mouton.

Hymes, Del, *On Communicative Competence,* University of Pennsylvania (forthcoming).

Inglis, F. (1969), *The Englishness of English Teaching,* Longman.

Inglis, F. (1971), 'How to do things with words: a critique of language studies', in *English in Education, Vol. 5., No. 2.* Chatto and Windus.

Jackson, B. and Denys Thompson (1962), *English in Education.* Chatto and Windus.

Johnson Abercrombie, M. L. (1960), *The Anatomy of Judgement,* Penguin 1960.

Jones, Richard (1972), *Fantasy and Feeling in Education,* Penguin.

Kelly, George (1963), *A theory of personality; The psychology of personal constructs,* W. W. Norton and Co, New York.

Leavis, F. R. (1943), *Education and the University,* Chatto and Windus.

91

Lyons, John (1968), *Introduction to Theoretical Linguistics,* Cambridge University Press.

Lyons, John, ed. (1970), *New Horizons in Linguistics,* Penguin.

Mead, George, H. (1934), *Mind, Self and Society,* University of Chicago Press.

Medawar, P. B. (1967), *The Art of the Soluble,* Methuen.

Medawar, P. B. (1969), *Induction and Intuition in Scientific Thought,* Methuen and Co Ltd.

Peters, R. S., ed. (1969), *Perspectives on Plowden,* Routledge and Kegan Paul.

Plowden (1967), *Children and their Primary Schools* (Plowden Report), H.M.S.O.

Polanyi, Michael (1958), *Personal Knowledge,* Routledge and Kegan Paul.

Popper, Karl (1963), *Conjectures and Refutations,* Routledge and Kegan Paul.

Postman, Neil and Charles Weingartner (1971), *Teaching as a subversive activity,* Penguin.

Richardson, Ken and David Spears (1972), *Race, Culture and Intelligence,* Penguin.

Roberts, Paul (1959), *Patterns of English,* Harcourt Brace.

Sprott, W. J. H. (1958), *Human Groups,* Penguin.

Sprott, W. J. H. (1970), 'Society, what is it and how does it change?' in ed. Swift, D. F., *Basic Readings in the Sociology of Education.* Routledge and Kegan Paul.

Whitehead, Frank (1966), *The Disappearing dais; a study of the principles and practices of English teaching,* Chatto and Windus.

Young, J. Z. (1971), *An Introduction to the Study of Man,* Oxford University Press.

Young, Michael, F. D. (1971), *Knowledge and Control,* Collier-Macmillan.

Appendix

Man's job/woman's work   F2

The goal of this unit is to show how a very familiar pattern in our vocabulary can reveal much about the attitude of our culture to what those words classify.

It takes as its starting point the fact that certain tasks are traditionally thought to be the prerogative of one sex or the other, and goes on to explore how the patterns of the vocabulary we use perpetuate these assumptions.

---

[1]   The aim of this session is to discover which tasks in the household are regarded as the man's job, and which the woman's. In discussion, consider such jobs as cooking, washing, washing-up, shopping, decorating, gardening, driving or washing the car, changing nappies, pushing the pram or mending fuses.
The discussion should look at the position of brothers and sisters, as well as fathers and mothers, and consider to what extent tensions arise where there is uncertainty as to who should do what within the family.

[2/3]   The aim of these sessions is to show that a number of words in the language carry with them the suggestion that particular jobs are properly performed by one sex or the other, and thereby show that such additional meanings are an essential part of the way language determines how we behave. This may be done in three ways:
   (a) by writing up the words Manager and Manageress, and asking the class to supply a list of organisations or institutions they may be found in charge of
   (b) by asking for examples of words which name jobs traditionally reserved for one sex, such as matron, au pair, jockey—or disc jockey. A variation of this is to write up a list of terms like 'con woman', 'charman' or 'night-

watchwoman' where the normal indications have been reversed

(c) by asking for words like mayor which usually connote one sex, but may be the other, and exploring the linguistic difficulties that follow.

[4] For this session, each member of the class should compile a list of names for jobs. By attempting to sort them into two simple lists, one clearly male, the other female, the class will discover that

(a) one term or the other has to be specially marked, as in doctor/lady doctor or nurse/male nurse

(b) a similar job has different labels, as in Air Steward/Air Hostess

(c) some pairs have a missing term, as in -/fishwife, -/tomboy, or wide boy/-

(d) in some related jobs, as in bus conductor/bus conductress and bus driver/-, a missing term may be significant.

The discussion will show how the resources of the language are exploited for this kind of labelling and consequently where the culture reveals itself in the gaps and special cases that occur.

This unit considers the way in which we use language simply to establish and maintain social contact with other people. What is said is much less important than the attitudes to the other person we indicate by our way of saying it.

The unit examines what happens in that common situation when two or three strangers are brought into contact with one another by chance, and shows how speech is used to avoid the awkwardness and unease of such a situation. The aim is to show pupils how such commonplace talk forms an essential part of the fabric of living.

---

[1]   In this session, the class should divide into small groups to prepare short sketches which will show what they think is likely to happen when a few people are thrown together in a situation where they feel impelled to say something. The sketches should be presented to the whole class. Before the last two groups present their sketches, they can be sent out of the room and the class asked to say what they expect them to talk about. In discussion, the class should consider why people talk at all in such a situation, why there seem to be almost set patterns of talk available to us for just these situations, and what would happen if no one talked at all. The situation needs to be a very simple one, like people gathering at a bus-stop, or sitting in a train much delayed, or being in the room while a repair is carried out.

[2] The aim of this session is to explore, again by using the small groups to prepare and present sketches, the kind of situation in which people feel that they have to keep talking because the situation requires it. Examples include car driver and hitch-hiker; cricket commentator during various intervals; guests at a wedding; preliminary to business meeting; receptionist greeting patient or candidate. After watching the sketches, the class should consider such questions as:

(a) what is the difference between talk
  (i) where the audience is limited to one or two (the hitch-hiker)
  (ii) where the audience may be only one person but the context is formal, public or social (the wedding)
  (iii) where the talk is merely preliminary.
(b) what subjects are not acceptable?
(c) what else are we conveying while talking and what are we discovering about other people?

[3] The aim of this session is to explore what happens when we want to break off social talk in a situation where the other person is determined to go on. Ask the groups to take up one of the sketches from [1] or [2] and add someone who does not know when to stop or who talks about a highly personal matter like losing his job, or assumes that his listeners share his political views. In discussion, the class should consider:
(a) how the others react
(b) how he can be stopped.
(c) why talk of this kind is unacceptable in the context
(d) why a person might talk in this way in an inappropriate context.